EVANGELICALISM
AND THE DECLINE OF
AMERICAN POLITICS

EVANGELICALISM
and the Decline of
AMERICAN POLITICS

Jan G. Linn

CASCADE *Books* · Eugene, Oregon

EVANGELICALISM AND THE DECLINE OF AMERICAN POLITICS

Cascade Books
An Imprint of Wipf and Stock Publishers
199 W. 8th Ave., Suite 3
Eugene, OR 97401

www.wipfandstock.com

PAPERBACK ISBN: 978-1-5326-0504-8
HARDCOVER ISBN: 978-1-5326-0506-2
EBOOK ISBN: 978-1-5326-0505-5

Cataloguing-in-Publication data:

Names: Linn, Jan G.

Title: Evangelicalism and the decline of American Politics / Jan G. Linn.

Description: Eugene, OR: Cascade Books, 2017 | Includes bibliographical references and index.

Identifiers: ISBN 978-1-5326-0504-8 (paperback) | ISBN 978-1-5326-0506-2 (hardcover) | ISBN 978-1-5326-0505-5 (ebook)

Subjects: LCSH: Evangelicalism. | Politics and government. | United States. | Title.

Classification: BR1642.U5 L57 2017 (print) | BR1642 (ebook)

Manufactured in the U.S.A.   SEPTEMBER 19, 2017

For my dad

A union man whose whole life was about social justice,
whose religious beliefs he kept to himself.

TABLE OF CONTENTS

ACKNOWLEDGMENTS

WRITING A BOOK IS at its most human level an act of "inner" community. This is because it cannot be done without drawing upon all the influences, ideas, and conversations that have contributed to shaping your worldview and how you see and respond to issues.

I cannot even begin to name or remember all the people whose own life and actions and points of view influenced my mind and heart in conscious and unconscious ways. What I do know is that, because of them, I have religious and political beliefs that give my life meaning, while also constantly stretching me in uncomfortable ways. Above all, those influences are why I believe as strongly as I do that religion and politics must live in tension with each other for either to matter.

The hard part is knowing how they live in tension without one compromising the other or becoming so impassioned about either or both to the point of going off the proverbial deep end. I credit the vivid memories of growing up in a family whose dinner table conversations always included the topics not suitable for polite company—religion and politics—to develop the courage to step close to the edge without going over. Of course, as Curly quipped in the film *City Slickers*, "day ain't over yet." Extremism is always a temptation, especially for people who care deeply about issues. It is the perpetual nemesis of reason and rationality. What has helped me thus far, I think, is learning early in life that religious and political beliefs are not the same as truth itself, preventing me from thinking that the world will end unless it listens to me.

I believe the marked decline in civility in our national debates about issues of importance is commensurate with the increased acceptability of extremism. This book is about how and why evangelical Christians have contributed to this problem. The challenge was trying to provide a "fair and balanced" (a phrase I have come to dislike immensely) analysis of the subject. To write about extremism creates feelings that mirror what you are writing about. My "salvation" has been other people who were able to recognize when I was stepping over the line and calling me on it, though they bear no responsibility for those places where I obviously ignored their counsel.

My indebtedness begins with a sizeable group of people who gather on Sundays in our home to discuss religion and politics, faith and reason, religious pluralism, and anything else a member of the group might bring up, all done in the context of worship. Because some are regulars and others move in and out, I will not try to name each of them. They know who they are, and the point of acknowledging them here is to express how very grateful I am for their presence in my life and in our weekly gatherings, their interest and encouragement in this book, and the numerous helpful comments they have made that have influenced the material in these pages.

Not above taking advantage of a friendship, I want to confess that I did so shamelessly with Bill Blackwell, a better friend than I deserve. Having grown up together, we have in our later adult years become best friends, a gift no one can merit, but can certainly treasure, despite the fact that we live a thousand miles apart. That is surely a testimony to the good side of social media. Not only is Bill smart and incredibly informed about the issues I discuss, he has to be the most competent unpaid copy editor in the world. More than that, he is a wordsmith whose style suggestions made parts of the book read so much better and with greater clarity than they would have. You can never repay friends, leaving the alternative to express appreciation to them. Thank you, Bill, not simply for your work on my behalf, but for your friendship.

If it were not enough that I take advantage of my friends, I also ask more of my wife, Joy, than I have a right to ask. It is, thus, with a heart overflowing with love that I inadequately express more often than not that I want to thank her for being willing to accept my being "absent" even as we would sit in the same room together, her knowing by the look in my eyes that I was still "writing" even though I had shut down the computer for the night. Like Bill, she read the material as I printed out the pages over and again, marking mistakes, and being willing to ask gently, "Are you sure this is what you want to say?" My mentor, Quaker scholar Elton Trueblood, was known to those of us who sat at his feet as "the encourager." That is the perfect way to describe Joy. Once in a while life deals us a good hand and we get better than we have any right to expect. Joy is that for me, the heart and soul of what it means to be the recipient of grace.

Finally, to my father to whom this book is dedicated. He taught me more by example than he ever knew by showing me in his work what doing for others truly means. His life was the labor movement, first as an organizer, then, for nearly thirty years a union representative for workers in the paper mill and textile industries. Having given his health and well being to serve them, he died a year after he took early retirement at the age of sixty-three. Every major labor leader I had ever heard of attended his funeral because, as they said of him, he was the best of the best. The CEOs of the companies where his union members worked also came or sent letters of condolence, calling him a man they respected for being tough, fair, and honest.

My father revered three persons in his life: FDR, union leader Walter Reuther, and God, in that order. When I was too young to know better I worried about his priorities. As I got older I realized that I had nothing to worry about, that my dad had only one priority—justice. Each of the names on that list was another way of expressing what he believed and believed in. He would be embarrassed had he heard me say that he set an example for a son who became a minister. He was too busy doing the very things I talk about more than do. There is no better example than that. That is why this book is for him.

PROLOGUE: THIS IS PERSONAL

THIS BOOK IS ABOUT people I know, people in my family, people I grew up with, went to school with, went to church with, people who believe things I once believed, people who are still friends of mine. I was teaching and serving as chaplain in my hometown of Lynchburg, Virginia in 1979 when Jerry Falwell founded the Moral Majority. For several years I got calls from reporters looking for information on Falwell they could use for a scoop of some sort. I was a prime choice for interviews because I grew up the neighborhood where he did. Some of his family attended the same church where my family belonged, and some of my family—uncles, aunts, and cousins—attended his church.

But I didn't learn about evangelicalism from Jerry Falwell. I was raised in it. My home church was the largest evangelical church in our city, actually the largest church period, long before Thomas Road Baptist Church came along. Falwell himself attended my church as a teenager, though he never acknowledged that in public as far as I know. I have heard evangelical theology all my life: God loved me; Jesus came to save me from my sins; I needed to accept Jesus into my heart and walk the straight and narrow way to get to heaven. I did as I was told and spent my adolescent and teen years singing gospel songs and trying my best to be good.

I also learned to love those old songs, and more than once was moved to tears as we sang "Tis Midnight, and on Olive's Brow" during the annual candlelight Maundy Thursday communion service. The story of Gethsemane, Jesus' trial before Pontius Pilate, and his walk to Golgotha was read, the sermon was preached, and the call to repentance was extended. People went forward to make the "Good Confession" of faith or to rededicate themselves to Jesus. Having combined Gethsemane and Good Friday at the candlelight service, we waited anxiously for Easter morning, when hundreds of us gathered for the sunrise service, and by Sunday school hour the number had swelled to a couple of thousand.

This was the evangelicalism of my youth and it remains evangelicalism for many Christians today. It is an emotional religion, filled with tears for the suffering that humanity caused Jesus to endure and the joy of knowing you have been saved from eternal damnation. All of it, then and now, is a set of beliefs, propositions that define the way of righteousness and by contrast the way of sin. The assurance of salvation summed up the content and goal of the evangelicalism of my home church, and it is not very different today. For some of us, though, to paraphrase the Apostle Paul, as children we spoke like an evangelical child, thought like an evangelical child, and reasoned like an evangelical child, but when we became adults, we put away evangelical things (1 Cor 13:11). Others did not, many of whom ended up becoming members of a collective evangelical constituency of the Republican Party. In short, they moved from the pew to the ballot box, bringing the certainty of their religious beliefs into partisan politics to the point where the federal government is virtually dysfunctional.

There is, as I will show, a very real and dangerous connection between Republican obstructionism in Washington and evangelical theology. Evangelicals do not consider any possibility that what they believe may be wrong. There is no shade of gray in their religious convictions or their worldview. There are right and wrong beliefs and they know which is which. After years of hearing recalcitrant Republicans in Congress talk the same way about their political views as I heard people in my home church talk about their religious beliefs, it became quite apparent that there is an uncanny parallel attitude and tone between the two that is hardly coincidental.

To give them credit, evangelical leaders told the rest of us what they planned to do. They would change America by taking over city councils, school boards, state houses, and eventually the US Congress. Having achieved many of those goals, politicians who consider themselves evangelical Christians are trying with all their political might to enact evangelical morality into law. What they have run into, though, is an American electorate that is as skeptical of evangelical preachers as it is of politicians. As a result evangelicals have not yet succeeded in indoctrinating most Americans to their way of thinking. You will see in the surveys noted in the pages to follow that evangelicalism's view of the world in most instances is not shared by a majority of the population. But that seems to be a challenge to evangelicals rather than a deterrent. In recent years they have been bearing down harder in finding ways to circumvent what most Americans want.

It is time to connect the dots between evangelicals as a Republican constituency and the breakdown of our political process. Not only does Washington no longer work, its tone has become mean and its policies more extreme. This book is about how and why Republican evangelicalism is a major reason this has happened. The political incivility that characterizes what is going on in Washington today certainly has history that precedes partisan evangelicalism, but the evidence is strong that it is worse than it has ever been and certainly worse than it would be had evangelicals not joined the Republican Party.

Some people, like Barry Goldwater, saw it coming and tried to tell other Republicans about it. They didn't listen and are now paying the price. But so is the entire nation, and that is why I decided a book like this needed to be written. There is no pleasure in exposing the dangers partisan evangelicals pose, but there is a sense of duty to what the rest of us believe, believe in, and want for our nation.

1

PARTISAN EVANGELICALISM

IN APRIL OF 2015, *World* magazine did a survey[1] of the nation's top 100 evangelical leaders to find out who was their preferred 2016 presidential candidate. 39 percent chose Marco Rubio as either their first or second choice, 32 percent named Jeb Bush as their first or second option, and Wisconsin Governor Scott Walker came in third with 28 percent.[2] The survey was taken before Donald Trump joined the race. But what stands out from the results of the survey is that no potential Democratic nominee was chosen by any of these evangelical leaders. No surprise there. Since the founding of the Moral Majority in 1979 that marked the end of evangelicals sitting on the sidelines of American politics, evangelical Christians have become "the Republican Party's largest and most reliable constituency."[3]

It is this partisan political reality that is the focus of this book, partly to expose the fact that evangelicals have played no small role in pushing the Republican Party to the far right, which in turn has resulted in our federal government being in a state of political dysfunction. Based on their words and actions, evangelicals have made it clear that the goal of their political actions is to shape the moral life of our country into their own image. Those moral convictions are grounded in theological beliefs they hold with absolute conviction. That in turn has led them to take a "no compromise" stand on moral issues, fearing as they do that compromise is a tool of liberals to convince the public to embrace moral relativism as a way of life.

1. Wuthnow, *Inventing American Religion*. Surveys provide a glimpse of views held at a given moment. The combination of several with similar results adds to their credibility. Wuthnow counsels caution, though as he shows how polls themselves exert considerable influence in shaping public opinion.

2. Bumpas, "What are evangelicals' thoughts on election issues?"

3. Mann and Ornstein, *It's Even Worse That It Looks*, 47.

Thus far evangelical Republicans have basked in their political power. But in the process they have also stirred the waters of controversy to the point where our political, racial, and social differences have evolved into divisions, our public discourse has become more uncivil, and our government has become dysfunctional in being able to bring differing political views to the table to make laws that work for the common good. Evangelicals are not the only reason for this state of affairs, but they have been a major player in it. That they have been involved at all in creating the worst political conflict and division we have seen in generations is enough to indict evangelicalism for its undermining of Christian values and Christian morals.

What is truly ironic is that it was Mr. Conservative himself, former Republican Senator from Arizona and 1964 presidential nominee, Barry Goldwater, who saw this coming.

> Mark my word, if and when these preachers get control of the [Republican] party, and they're sure trying to do so, it's going to be a terrible damn problem. Frankly, these people frighten me. Politics and governing demand compromise. But these Christians believe they are acting in the name of God, so they can't and won't compromise. I know, I've tried to deal with them.[4]

While Goldwater's views moderated over time, *Washington Post* columnist E. J. Dionne contends in his book, *Why the Right Went Wrong*, that Goldwater's presidential nomination in 1964 marked the beginning of the Republican Party's turn to the radical right, in large part because it ushered in an era that continues today wherein conservative politicians continue to make promises to their supporters that they cannot keep.[5] Goldwater himself, as Dionne reminds us, opened the door in his presidential run to the very evangelicals he later came to see as a threat to the Republican Party. Goldwater's goal was to turn "the interplay between morality, race, and crime into political capital," but he lived to regret it.[6] In Salt Lake City Goldwater pledged "my effort to a reconstruction of reverence and moral strength, those great pillars of human happiness in our land." He went on to criticize his opponent, President Lyndon Johnson, for ensuring that the Democratic Party platform made no reference to God or religion.[7] It was only later that the seeds of intraparty chaos he himself had planted grew

4. "Quote of the Day."
5. Dionne, *Why the Right Went Wrong*, 3–4.
6. Ibid., 56.
7. Ibid., 57.

into a "terrible damned problem" that is now not only threatening the viability of the Republican Party, but the entire American political system. In order to understand the degree of the crisis we are in and the role evangelicalism is playing in it, we need first to look extensively at the facts that support the claim that the responsibility for the degree of dysfunction we are seeing in Washington today lies with the Republican Party.

The power of the radical right among Republicans is widely believed to have been a major factor in former Speaker of the House John Boehner giving up his position along with his seat in Congress. It became too frustrating for him to face the seemingly impossible task of getting the various factions of the Republican-controlled House of Representatives to work together enough to pass needed legislation. Without fail, one or another of them would make unyielding and at times outrageous demands that had to be met. In the end they got rid of Boehner, who they never considered a genuine friend to their causes, and then defeated the bid of Representative Kevin McCarthy of California to replace Boehner. They finally agreed to support Representative Paul Ryan of Wisconsin as Speaker because of his ultra-conservative economic policies, even though he had not expressed any desire to have the position.

The story of what has happened to the Republican Party is effectively told in the book *It's Even Worse Than It Looks*, coauthored by Thomas Mann and Norman Ornstein. Mann is a respected congressional scholar at the liberal Brookings Institute. Ornstein is a founding member of the influential conservative think tank, the American Enterprise Institute. They wrote the book in order "to clarify the source of dysfunctional politics and what it will take to change it."[8]

In their earlier book, *The Broken Branch*, published in 2006, they had laid bare the extreme partisanship in Congress that had led to their conclusion that it was broken.

> We documented the demise of regular order, as Congress bent rules to marginalize committees and deny the minority in the House opportunities to offer amendments on the floor; the decline of genuine deliberation in the law making process on such important matters as budgets and decisions to go to war; the manifestations of extreme partisanship; the culture of corruption; the loss

8. Mann and Ornstein, *It's Even Worse than It Looks,* xiii.

of institutional patriotism among members; and the weakening of the checks and balances system.[9]

But in the six years following the publication of that book they reached another conclusion, that the political dysfunction in Washington had become much worse because of Republican obstructionism. What they call "asymmetrical polarization" had emerged, wherein Republicans clearly bore more responsibility for government dysfunction than Democrats. As they put it:

> However awkward it may be for the traditional press and nonpartisan analysts to acknowledge, the Republican Party has become an insurgent outlier—ideologically extreme, contemptuous of the inherited and social and economic policy regime; scornful of compromise, unpersuaded by conventional understanding of facts, evidence, and science; and dismissive of the legitimacy of its political opposition. When one party moves this far from the center of American politics, it is extremely difficult to enact policies responsive to the country's most pressing challenges.[10]

Dionne also documents this asymmetrical polarization when he cites a Pew Research Center survey that asked Democrats and Republicans if they preferred elected officials who were willing to make compromises with people they disagreed with or officials who would stick to their positions unyieldingly. Fifty-nine percent of Democrats preferred compromise officials, but only thirty-six percent of Republicans did.[11] But Mann, Ornstein, and Dionne are not alone in their assessments of what has happened to Republicans. Republican David Frum, advisor to George W. Bush, wrote in 2014 that the American political right had "veered toward a reactionary radicalism unlike anything seen in American party politics in modern times."[12] Republicans, of course, blame President Obama for Washington dysfunction, but Dionne underscores the fact that the evidence points to just the opposite conclusion:

> Obama certainly had his shortcomings. But to assume that Obama was ever in a position to build broad support among Republicans for his program ignores their determination, from the very first day of his presidency, to prevent progressive policies from

9. Ibid., xi.

10. Ibid., xiv.

11. Ibid., 12.

12. Frum, "Don't Knock the Reform Conservatives."

taking hold. More effective schmoozing and more invitations to the White House might have been nice, but they would not have solved Obama's problem. The fierceness of the opposition he faced had deep structural and historical roots in the long-term changes in conservatism and in the Republican Party.[13]

It is this kind of informed analysis of what is going on in Washington that undercuts claims that reflect a "false equivalency" promoted by Republicans and accepted even by some independents. Worse, though, it reveals a fundamental failure to understand how serious the crisis that we are facing as a nation is. The truth is that no political party has ever reached the point of wanting the government not to function at all until now, but this is where the Republican Party is today.

New York Times conservative political columnist David Brooks ascribes the state of American politics to an "antipolitics" attitude that is most clearly, though not exclusively, embodied in the Tea Party. People who are antipolitics, he says, "want to elect people who have no political experience. They want 'outsiders.' They delegitimize compromise and deal-making. They're willing to trample the customs and rules that give legitimacy to legislative decision-making if it helps them gain power." Ultimately, he contends, "they don't recognize other people. They suffer from a form of political narcissism, in which they don't accept the legitimacy of other interests and opinions. They don't recognize restraints. They want total victories for themselves and their doctrine." The consequences of this antipolitics attitude, Brooks says, is that it "has had a wretched impact on our democracy."[14]

Former Virginia Republican Lt. Governor Bill Bolling said publicly that the antipolitics attitude Brooks was talking about has become so extreme that the Republican Party no longer understands that being conservative is not the same thing as being anti-government.[15] When Republican anti-tax zealot Grover Norquist made the comment, "I don't want to abolish government. I simply want to reduce it to the size where I can drag it into the bathroom and drown it in the bathtub,"[16] he confirmed precisely what Brooks and Bolling were saying.

13. Dionne, *Why the Right Went Wrong*, 4.

14. Brooks, "The Governing Cancer of Our Time,"

15. Bolling, "What to call a do-something conservative?"

16. Liasson, "Conservative Advocate."

In the making for years, this radicalization of the Republican Party finally reared its ugly head immediately after President Obama's 2009 inauguration. Former Ohio Senator George Voinovich described the strategy Republican Minority Leader Mitch McConnell presented to the Senate Republican caucus at the time this way: "If he [Obama] was for it, we had to be against it. He [McConnell] wanted everyone to hold the fort. All he cared about was making sure Obama could never have a clean victory."[17]

A stunning example of what Voinovich said involved a deficit reduction proposal in 2010. Because of the contentiousness between themselves and President Obama from the beginning of his presidency over reducing the federal deficit, Democrat Kent Conrad of North Dakota and Republican Judd Greg of New Hampshire coauthored a resolution to create an eighteen-member deficit-reduction task force that would have the power to fast-track a procedure to bring a significant plan for deficit reduction straight to the Senate floor for an up-or-down vote.

The measure had strong bipartisan support, including Senator John McCain of Arizona, a cosponsor, and Mitch McConnell of Kentucky, who made a plea to President Obama in a Senate speech urging him to support the proposal. Yet Republicans chose to filibuster the bill and when the Senate tried to break it, Senators like McCain and McConnell and six other original cosponsors of the bill all voted to sustain it. Mann and Ornstein point out that this was the first time in history that cosponsors of a major bill voted against their own idea. What reason did Republicans have for doing such a thing? "Because President Barack Obama was for it, and its passage might give him political credit."[18]

A year later the Republican Chairman of the House Transportation and Infrastructure Committee, Representative John Mica, chose to put the safety of the American public at risk to force President Obama to accept his openly partisan economic demands for the Federal Aviation Agency (FAA). He issued a set of demands to the Democratically controlled Senate with the note that they were "non-negotiable." First, he demanded a provision be inserted in the FAA reauthorization act that would eliminate collective bargaining rights for FAA workers that other federal employees had. The other was a provision to cut subsidies to small airports, all of which were located in Democratic states and districts. When his demands were not met, the FAA partially shut down and put the traveling public at real risk.

17. Grunwald, "The Party of No."
18. Mann and Ornstein, *It's Even Worse than It Looks*, x.

Thousands of workers were furloughed, airplane inspectors were forced to pay their own travel expenses, work on airport and runway renovations and construction was halted, throwing 24,000 people out of work, and the FAA could not collect airfare taxes that ended up costing the government $300 million in lost revenue that was a larger amount than any savings there would have been if small airports subsidies had been cut.[19]

During his entire tenure, President Obama confronted this wall of obstructionism, at first when Senate Republicans chose to use the filibuster as their primary tool of obstructionism, and later when they gained control of the Senate altogether. Before dysfunction became the rule of the day the filibuster was a legislative procedure that had been used sparingly. Today it is used regularly, having been employed on average some 140 times a legislative session, and often when Senate sessions have been the shortest in history.

One of the reasons the public doesn't hear about filibusters is the Senate rule called "holds" that allows one person to indicate in private that he or she will filibuster a measure if it is brought to the floor. "Holds" have allowed filibusters to be done quietly to avoid public exposure. They have also become the de facto replacement for the constitutionally mandated simple majority vote requirement for legislation to pass. Now a sixty-vote supermajority is required to reach cloture, meaning overriding a "hold." Because of the Republican strategy of obstructionism in the Senate it is now at the point, as one person put it, where anything more controversial than renaming a post office requires a supermajority just to get a vote. So it is no surprise that "the correct count of how many bills have been filibustered during Obama's presidency is, approximately all of them."[20]

This is why President Obama's nominations for his own cabinet had to wait weeks and even months before being voted on, and for no reason at all. His judicial nominations fared even worse. Republicans filibustered or refused to consider more of President Obama's executive branch and judicial nominees than all the nominations made by all other presidents combined. One egregious example of the kind of obstructionism he faced was Judge Robert Bacharach of Oklahoma. Nominated to the Tenth Circuit Court of Appeals, Bacharach was supported by the state's two conservative Oklahoma Republicans, then Senator Tom Coburn and Senator Jim Inhofe, and was not opposed by any other Republican Senator. Yet Republicans

19. Ibid., 81–82.
20. Bernstein, "All Filibusters, All the Time."

filibustered his confirmation for almost nine months, and when they finally allowed a vote he was approved unanimously.

Attorney General Loretta Lynch's nomination went through a similar kind of arbitrary delay by Republicans. Prior to being nominated she had distinguished herself as US Attorney for the Eastern District of New York for being a competent, tough, and effective prosecutor, winning praise from the American Bar Association and colleagues as eminently qualified to be Attorney General. No matter, Republicans held up the vote on her nomination for over five months. When she was finally approved it was by a fifty-six to forty-three margin that included ten Republicans voting in her favor.

Once Republicans gained control of the Senate, Majority Leader Mitch McConnell controlled the agenda to the point where virtually everything Democrats proposed remained in limbo, including most of President Obama's judicial nominations. Obama's nomination of Merrick B. Garland to fill the Supreme Court vacancy left by the sudden death of Justice Antonin Scalia in February of 2016 never even got a hearing. When nominated, Garland was Chief Judge of the US Court of Appeals for the District of Columbia, the most important Circuit Court in the nation, where he had gained a reputation as a fair, impartial, and thoughtful judge whose overall voting record placed him neither right nor left. In spite of the fact that a CNN/ORC International poll taken in March of 2016 found that two-thirds of all Americans believed that hearings should be held and a vote taken on the Merrick Garland nomination,[21] McConnell persisted in refusing to allow any action on his nomination. The true irony of his actions was that he claimed he wanted to give the American people a say in appointment through the 2016 presidential election results. Apparently McConnell did not believe the polls that showed most Americans did not support his position or that Barack Obama's reelection in 2012 by more than five million votes was the voice of the American people speaking.

This kind of rancor has not only kept important legislation from being considered, cabinet and ambassador positions going unfilled, and seats left unfilled on federal courts across the country, it has also put the full faith and credit of our government at risk. In 2011 Republicans threatened to filibuster raising the debt limit that would allow the government to pay for appropriations it had already made unless Obama agreed to major cuts in the budget, including the repeal of his signature legislative achievement, the Affordable Healthcare Act (Obamacare). The conflict was finally resolved

21. Agiesta, "Support for SCOTUS hearings remains strong."

without Republicans getting their way, but immediately afterwards the credit rating agency Standard & Poor's downgraded the credit rating of the United States from its AAA status for the first time in our nation's history. It cited the government getting to the brink of defaulting on its debts as the reason for its action. Downgrades were also made after Standard & Poor's by other credit agencies because of the continuing brinksmanship by Republicans that finally led to Republicans shutting down the government in 2013 for three-and-a-half weeks. In years past raising the debt ceiling was perfunctory because the ceiling itself is a self-imposed arbitrary limit set by the government and no party had ever before used raising it as a bargain chip in budget disputes. Now it has become a routine Republican threat.

E. J. Dionne describes the "crash and burn" approach Republicans are employing this way: "If it cannot take power, the GOP is committed, on principle, to preventing its adversaries from governing successfully."[22] He further argues that the fight over Obamacare that shut down the government underscored just how far radical right Republicans have moved, given the fact that it is a market-based approach to healthcare reform promoted by the conservative think tank the Heritage Foundation, and was essentially the same plan put forth by Republicans in the mid-'90s as an alternative to the Clinton proposal.[23] The behavior of today's Republicans has reached the point where, according to Geoffrey Kabaservice, moderates in the party, if not extinct, are becoming endangered. "If American politics can be compared to an ecosystem," he says, "then the disappearance of the moderate Republicans represents a catastrophic loss of species diversity."[24] What Kabaservice suggests has in fact been confirmed on several occasions as Republicans Senators and Representatives considered "mainstream" have gone down in defeat in primary contests, none more shocking than the 2014 defeat of Eric Cantor, House Minority Whip at the time, to Tea Party candidate Dave Brat.

There are, of course, dissident voices that take issue with describing what is happening in American politics today. Actually Mann and Ornstein acknowledge some of them,[25] if only to underscore the point that the primary issue we are facing is not about one party using the filibuster more

22. Dionne, *Why the Right Went Wrong,* 6.
23. Ibid., 421.
24. Yardley, "Rule and Ruin."
25. Mann and Ornstein, *It's Worse than It Looks,* 110.

than the other. It is, instead, about the degree to which Republicans are using legislative rules to stop anything from getting done. In their words:

> These perilous times and the political responses to them are qualitatively different from what we have seen before. There is no guarantee that the country's troubles will be short-lived and the political system self-correcting. Indeed, the magnitude of the problems in the wake of the most severe economic crisis since the 1930s and the difficulty other democracies are experiencing in trying to mitigate its devastating effects should strengthen America's resolve to fix its dysfunctional politics.[26]

Former Nebraska Republican Senator Chuck Hagel agrees. He described the 2013 government shutdown engineered by Republicans as "an astounding lack of leadership by many in the Republican Party," adding, "I think the Republican Party is captive to political movements that are very ideological, that are very narrow."[27] Recall as well the assessment of what has happened to Republicans by former Republican Lt. Governor of Virginia Bill Bolling, mentioned earlier in this chapter. When he first ran for office in 2005 Bolling said he was considered a conservative Republican. Now he is being called an "establishment" Republican, yet he says, "my political philosophy and approach is the same today as it has always been, but the definition of what it means to be a conservative Republican has obviously changed."[28] Bolling says one of the main differences between the kind of conservative Republican he is and the new kind of conservative is that he believes being conservative is not the same as being anti-government, nor does it mean you cannot respect people who disagree with your philosophy of government.

But what troubles Bolling the most is that today "it is not enough to have a conservative political philosophy and approach . . . it is more about style than substance." So what passes for being a "true" conservative Republican requires accepting three traits he finds very distasteful:

> First, you must adhere to a rigid and sometimes extreme conservative political philosophy.
> Second, you must adamantly oppose and demonize those that do not fully agree with you on every issue.

26. Ibid.,111.
27. Ibid., 54.
28. Bolling, "What to call a do-something conservative?"

Third, you must take an absolutist, and often times mean-spirited approach to politics and policy.[29]

Bolling's final comment is especially noteworthy. He is convinced that conservatives who promote a mean-spirited approach to politics and policy now have major influence in the Republican Party. Because they do a decorum of good will and genuine concern for the common good are gone. These conservatives prevent any steps being taken by either side to help our political process regain its balance. They have no will for the government to function better. They simply don't want it to function at all unless they control what it does. This is what happens when people with an absolutist attitude gain power.

This brings us full circle to the "serious damned problem" evangelicalism has become for Republicans and for the entire American political process. As visible as evangelicals are, though, it is more than a little difficult to determine a consensus among them about what makes someone "evangelical," a reality underscored by Corwin Smidt's book, *American Evangelicalism Today*. Definitions of evangelicalism matter, he insists, not least because the diversity of views on the subject has led to estimates of how many Americans are evangelical in faith that range from 10 percent to 40 percent. He prefers to define evangelicals as members of a religious *tradition* rather than a religious *movement*,[30] with "membership" in a tradition being determined by one's self-identification with a particular denomination or, in the case of most Black Protestants, with certain nondenominational evangelical churches.[31]

In contrast to Smidt, historian Molly Worthen takes the *movement* approach in defining evangelicalism. She suggests that the most effective way to understand who evangelicals are is to ask three basic questions:

Evangelicals are Protestants who since the aftermath of the Reformation have been circling around three questions. Those questions are: First, how do you reconcile faith and reason? How do you maintain one coherent way of knowing? Second, how do you become sure of your salvation? How do you meet Jesus and develop a relationship with him, to use the language that some

29. Ibid.
30. Smidt, *American Evangelicals Today*, xii.
31. Ibid., xiii.

evangelicals prefer. And third, how do you reconcile your personal
faith with an increasingly pluralistic, secular public sphere?[32]

Focusing on these questions, she says, allows a wider and more diver-
gent range of Christian groups/denominations to be seen as "evangelical,"
but her view has met with resistance precisely because of its broadness.
Others prefer the slightly less expansive definition suggested by historian
David Bebbington several years ago that has since become known as "the
Bebbington Quadrilateral." It consists of these four things:

> Biblicism: a high regard for the Bible
> Crucicentrism: a focus on Jesus's crucifixion and its saving effects
> Conversionism: a belief that humans need to be converted
> Activism: the belief that faith should influence one's public life[33]

On the surface the "Bebbington Quadrilateral" seems to provide basic
touchstone points in understanding the meaning of modern evangelicalism, but it is also general enough to allow different and divergent explana-
tions of what these four statements mean. The devil, it seems, really is in
the details. A high regard for the Bible, for example, might be interpreted to
mean believing it contains the word of God when evangelicals actually believe the Bible is the word of God. Those are two very different approaches
to the Bible, yet the "Bebbington Quadrilateral" seems to allow one to go
either way. It also seems to open the door to differing views of what "crucicentrism" means. Are "the saving effects" of Jesus' death the same thing
as sacrificial atonement? Or do other concepts of atonement also define
evangelicalism? If so that may come as a surprise to many evangelicals.
What about "conversionism"? Does that mean becoming a Christian is a
necessity, especially in light of "crucicentrism," or is conversion an act of
joining a church? Finally, does "activism" extend beyond your own life to
"making disciples of all nations"?

The "Bebbington Quadrilateral" intentionally describes evangelical
beliefs in a less rigid form than is often the case, making it possible for
someone like Chine Mbubaegbu, the first woman to become director of
communications for the Worldwide Evangelical Alliance in 2014, to think
of evangelicalism as do members of Evangelicals for Social Action. Upon
being named to her position, Mbubaegbu cautioned evangelicals to be
careful about how they communicate what it means to be who they are.

32. Stanley, "The Intellectual Civil War within Evangelicalism."
33. Merritt, "Defining 'Evangelical.'"

The perception the public has of evangelicals, she said, is that they are ho-mophobic, judgmental, woman-hater people. She believes they can present themselves as the opposite of this image:

> When the word evangelical is used in any other context, it simply means someone who is passionate about a certain thing and is keen that everyone knows about it. That's what I want evangeli-cals to be known for: being passionate followers of Christ, keen on seeing his good news impact every area of society—with our hearts turned towards those facing injustice or who are forgotten and excluded.[34]

Whether or not as communications director she can change the public image of evangelicalism remains a great challenge, not least because many of its leaders promote the very image of evangelicals she wants to dispel. Russell Moore, President of the Ethics & Religious Liberty Commission of the Southern Baptist Convention, insists that evangelicalism is not about social justice, but about salvation through Jesus Christ. In a *Washington Post* article he wrote in 2016 he sounded nothing like Chine Mbubaegbu or the "Bebbington Quadrilateral" in what he said about evangelicalism. Carrying the title "Why this election makes me hate the word 'evangeli-cal'," Moore lamented the fact that so many evangelicals were supporting Donald Trump for president and thereby were contradicting what it means to be one.

> The word "evangelical" isn't, first of all, about American politics. The word is rooted in the Greek word for gospel, good news for sinners through the life, death, resurrection and reign of Jesus of Nazareth as the son of God and anointed ruler of the cosmos. . . . Evangelical means a commitment to the truth of God's revelation in the Bible and a conviction that the blood of Christ is offered to any repentant, believing sinner as a full atonement for sin.[35]

Trump supporters, he said, were "rending the word 'evangelical' . . . almost meaningless" to the point where "the word itself is . . . subverting the gospel of Jesus Christ."[36] The criticism of Trump supporters aside, Moore clearly understands evangelicalism with a serious degree of specificity that does not suggest leeway outside the lines he has drawn. For him evangeli-

---

34. Woods, "Evangelicalism is not about homophobia or hating women."
35. Wehner, "Why this elections makes me hate the word 'evangelical.'"
36. Ibid.

calism is about Jesus as savior of the world and ruler of the whole universe. It is about the need to believe this is true because the Bible as the revealed word of God declares that the atoning death of Jesus is the only means of divine forgiveness. In short, I suspect without intending to do so Moore explained why evangelicals are not only seen as judgmental and homophobic, but in fact are.

What is found on the website "What Evangelical Christians Believe Project" offers a similar understanding of evangelicalism as Moore's. It describes itself as "a collaborative effort by numerous groups, churches, and evangelical organizations to achieve a consensus on fundamental evangelical beliefs." Eleven beliefs constitute that consensus definition:

1. Bible. We believe that the Bible is the Word of God; without error as originally written. Its content has been preserved by Him, and is the final authority in all matters of doctrine and faith—above all human authority.

2. God. We believe there is no God but one: the infinite Designer, Creator, and Sustainer of all existence in this or any universe—from eternity past to eternity future. God's nature is triune—three perfect and eternal persons; Father, Son, and Holy Spirit—who are one, in being as well as in purpose.

3. Law. We believe God is the source of all moral and natural law. The highest and all-encompassing law, given to man, is to love the one true God above all else.

4. Man. We believe that man is a created, finite being; designed in the image of God, with the ability to reason, make choices, and have relationships. Man was created for the purpose of bringing glory to God, but since the day man first rebelled against God's law, all mankind has been sinful by nature, and has earned the penalty of death and eternal separation from God.

5. Jesus. We believe that God, the Son, entered the world as a man to die on the cross on our behalf; a sinless sacrifice in full payment of all our sin—both past and future—satisfying the demand of God's perfect justice. Jesus rose from the grave; authenticating His divine identity, as our living Prophet, Priest, and King.

6. Forgiveness. Based upon the penalty paid at the cross, we believe that the forgiveness of sins is granted by grace alone to those who will

receive it by faith alone. It must be received as an utterly undeserved gift or it cannot be received at all; because all the credit and glory are Christ's alone.

7. Repentance. We turn (repent) from self-reliance for our salvation, to trusting alone in the completed work of Jesus upon the cross to purchase the perfect pardon of all our sin, forever.

8. Works. We believe in doing good works in grateful response to our pardon, not to cause it. From our faith, acts of response will flow such as: obedience, compassion, baptism, communion, prayer, etc.

9. Inheritance. As believers, we are Christ's true church, and have consequently received many other spiritual blessings, including: reconciliation and friendship with a Holy God, the indwelling of the Holy Spirit, adoption as children of God into His family, and eternal life now and in His kingdom.

10. Deception. We also acknowledge the existence of the great counterfeiter of prophecy, miracles, emotions, and feelings: Satan. Therefore, we take seriously God's command to test all these things according to scripture.[37]

Evangelical scholar Mark Noll argues that that "evangelicalism has always been made up of shifting movements, temporary alliances, and the lengthened shadows of individuals." He goes on to add, "All discussions of evangelicalism, therefore, are always both descriptions of the way things really are as well as efforts within our own minds to provide some order for a multifaceted, complex set of impulses and organizations."[38] What Noll is indirectly referring to is the long and in many respects distinguished history of evangelical thinking that pre-existed what he says was the devastating impact of later–nineteenth-century fundamentalism on the evangelical mind (more about that in chapter five). For the moment all these various descriptions and definitions of evangelical beliefs makes pinpointing what evangelicalism is and who represents it dependent upon many variables.

This was the dilemma the respected conservative survey organization the Barna Group wanted to address. Frustrated by the wide variety of evangelical beliefs, they decided to do a survey seeking answers to nine specific

37. Evangelicalbeliefs.com.
38. Noll, *The Scandal of the Evangelical Mind*, 8.

faith questions to see what consensus they might find. Below are the basic beliefs they found that define who evangelicals really are.

> They have made a personal commitment to Jesus Christ that is still important in their life today . . . their faith is very important in their life today; [they believe] that when they die they will go to Heaven because they have confessed their sins and accepted Jesus Christ as their Savior . . . they have a personal responsibility to share their religious beliefs about Christ with non-Christians . . . [they believe] that Satan exists [and] that eternal salvation is possible only through grace, not works . . . that Jesus Christ lived a sinless life on earth . . . that the Bible is accurate in all the principles it teaches . . . and [they describe] God as the all-knowing, all-powerful, perfect deity who created the universe and still rules it today.[39]

These statements ring true because they are empirically based. They certainly reflect what I was taught to believe by my evangelical home church. More than that, I am confident that they are what evangelical church members hear on Sundays, and during election seasons those beliefs form the basis for what are told they *should* believe about the moral issues of today and candidates they *should* support.

There are, to be sure, evangelicals who are committed to peace and justice and especially helping the poor. Evangelicals for Social Action has gained respect among progressive Christians for putting social justice at the forefront of evangelical ethics, but the group in fact arose in 1974 out of the vacuum within evangelicalism whose sole focus up to that time was personal salvation. When George W. Bush used the phrase "compassionate conservative" to described himself as an evangelical Christian during the 2000 presidential campaign he was tapping into to this social justice side of evangelicalism. But his policies as president reflected a lot more "conservatism" and a lot less "compassion" than he suggested would be the case. Bush relied on private charity for the "compassion" he said he felt for people in need, choosing to be thoroughly Republican in trying to limit the role of government in helping those marginalized by social and economic realities.

Indeed, the Bush administration in actuality embodied more than most people realize everything that can go wrong when politicians use religion to their advantage and blur the line between democracy and theocracy. Journalist Esther Kaplan tells the story in stunning detail in her

39. "Barna Group survey exposes."

superbly researched book, *With God On Their Side: George W. Bush and the Christian Right*. A primary means by which this was done took the form of funding evangelical programs that formed the core of Bush's Faith-Based Initiative, an effort to replace government-sponsored social safety net programs with private services. In the end it turned out to be the government providing the financial basis for religious outreach programs that promoted evangelical beliefs theologically and socially, specifically those related to contraception and the treatment of AIDS patients. Kaplan quotes one prominent Boston minister who described Bush's Faith-Based Initiative as "a financial watering hole for the right-wing white evangelicals."[40]

All of this is to say that even when evangelicals claim to want to help people in need they seldom, if ever, do so without strings attached that reflect their moralistic and theological beliefs. Part of the reason this is the case is their evangelistic zeal to convert the world to Jesus Christ. If Jesus is the only begotten son of God (John 3:16) and the savior of the world, repentance of sin is a requisite for being saved from hell and for heaven. This message is seen as "good news" that evangelicals must spread, following the mandate they find in what is called the Great Commission given by Jesus: "All authority in heaven and on earth has been given to me. Go therefore and make disciples of all nations, baptizing them in the name of the Father and of the Son and of the Holy Spirit, and teaching them to obey everything that I have commanded you. And remember, I am with you always, to the end of the age" (Matt 28:18–20).

This evangelistic imperative is captured in the purpose statement of the "What Evangelical Christians Believe Project" as stated on its website: "Our desire for others is that they might be saved from the penalty and power of their sins, and, as a result, enjoy a personal and joyful relationship with their Creator forever. This happens when a person places their trust only and completely in the one true God for the free gift of a full and legal pardon—based upon the death of Jesus on the cross as their substitute."[41]

To understand evangelicalism you have to recognize the passion evangelicals have for evangelism. They are convinced that they are to use any means available, including politics, to remake the world in its own image. Perhaps no one exemplified this fact more than evangelical anti-feminist leader Phyllis Schlafly. Her book *The Power of The Christian Woman* is a candid statement about what she believed the Bible says about men and

40. Kaplan, *With God on Their Side*, 63.

41. Evangelicalbeliefs.com.

women, marriage and family, views that were the driving force behind her staunch Republican Party activism since the days of Barry Goldwater. Indeed, she may have been evangelicalism's most persistent and influential Republican crusader of the modern era.

Largely known for her successful defeat of the Equal Rights Amendment, and indirectly Betty Friedman and Gloria Steinem who led the effort to have it ratified, Schlafly was an advocate for a radical right moral/ traditional family political agenda as a member of the Republican Party for fifty years. Not all conservative women were drawn to Schlafly's views of the fight women must wage, as Rebecca Klatch highlights in her book, *Women of the New Right: Women in the Political Economy*. Klatch distinguishes social conservative new right women from those she identifies as "laissez-faire" new right women. The latter, she says, "measures the world according to the political and economic liberty of the individual," and "believes the primary element of society is the rational, self-interested individual."[42] In contrast, the social conservative woman's world is rooted in religious belief, Klatch says, that makes all perception colored by religious values.[43] Thus, the social conservative woman's world "is constructed around a divinely ordained hierarchy of authority; it is an integrated moral community based on the complementarity of male and female roles."[44]

The social conservative world is the source of the 50,000 women who have been attracted to Schlafly's crusade for biblically based family values in America through her organization, Eagle Forum, founded in 1972. The website is a literal smorgasbord of radical right conservative causes, including a barrage of Schlafly blogs explaining why homosexuality and same-sex marriage are a direct threat to biblically based families, why immigration threatens our security and our way of life, why the elimination of Christianity is a direct goal of Democrats, why mothers need to be in the home and fathers need to be head of the family, why feminism continues to be a threat to women, and numerous other evangelical causes.

Because of the number of women who support the Eagle Forum it is a formidable political force for Republicans, but it also represents just as powerful a force against any Republican who strays from the straight and narrow conservative religious and political views Schlafly held. Her endorsement of Donald Trump's candidacy before he secured the Republican

42. Klatch, *Women of the New Right*, 4.

43. Ibid.

44. Ibid., 53.

nomination underscored just how influential Schlafly was. Not that her word was accepted without pushback. Her Trump endorsement ignited a firestorm of resistance in the Eagle Forum, including from her own daughter, who joined other board members in an effort to remove the ninety-three-year-old Schlafly as CEO.

Schlafly was a powerful example of the way evangelical religious beliefs inform and shape evangelical political beliefs. A Republican before she became a moral crusader, she helped to make the case to evangelicals that they are engaged in war between forces of good and the forces of evil to save America's soul. But "religious" wars often make for strange bedfellows and even more enigmatic enemies. This showed itself to be the case for partisan evangelicalism right from the start. The person at whom they launched their first salvos was former President Jimmy Carter, who was probably the most sincerely Christian man ever to occupy the White House. His first sin was doing an interview that was published in *Playboy* magazine and earned him evangelical scorn. He then chose to be too honest for their taste in explaining that while he personally did not believe in abortion, as President he was bound by the Supreme Court decision that made choice a legal right. In a world of black and white, right and wrong, ambiguity cannot be tolerated. So evangelicals turned to Ronald Reagan, a decent man but hardly a paragon of virtue, as their candidate because he was anti-abortion and was for small government, which evangelicals took to mean he would resist any more efforts to "kick God out of schools."

Ever since evangelicalism chose to be partisan in its political participation it has gradually lost any capacity to offer a prophetic critique of Republican policies, consumed as it has been with using the political process to legislate its personal moral agenda. As a result, beyond the weakened voice of Evangelicals for Social Action, the evangelical movement has been focused almost exclusively on sex issues. When the worst economic crisis since the Great Depression of the 1930s hit in 2008, evangelicals remained loyal Republicans instead of helping the nation face the fundamental causes of it. It was no secret that the Bush tax cuts that benefited the very wealthy more than anyone else failed to stimulate the economy as promised. Adding to the impending catastrophe was the "off the books" unfunded wars of choice in Afghanistan and Iraq whose costs have now run into the trillions of dollars. If that were not enough, a Medicare Part D drug program that was intended for good turned out to be economically bad for the country. Not only was it unfunded, but forbid competitive price bidding that could have helped the government get the best deal it could. Added to these mistakes was the US overreaction to 9/11 that led our nation into an unprecedented build up of Homeland Security that saw literally billions of dollars wasted.[45]

With few exceptions, through all of these events evangelicals and evangelical institutions were silent. In 2004 their efforts to reelect President Bush made it clear that not even wars of choice could weaken their support for Republican candidates. What mattered most to them was being a political friend to the evangelical moral agenda. Of course, not every evangelical is a Republican, nor a zealot against abortion or homosexuality. But we know a large majority of them are by their voting record. Lydia Bean notes in her book *The Politics of Evangelical Identity* that white evangelicals have remained remarkably consistent in their Republican voting patterns. "In 2004, 77.5 percent supported the Republican candidate for president, and their support for the Republican Party was largely unchanged in 2008, 2010, and 2012."[46] At the same time, Bean argues that evangelicals here in the US (compared to Canadian evangelicals) are not bound to political conservatism because of their theology. Rather, she says, it is their ability to delegitimize political diversity among them.[47]

I suggest the comparison she makes between American and Canadian, while informative, leads her to a conclusion that contradicts both empirical and objective evidence. Evangelical moral beliefs are grounded in what they believe the Bible says. This is why "proof texting" is a primary tool employed by the majority in evangelical congregations to intimidate minority views that contradict the political consensus. Surveys suggest that moral beliefs are the key factor in why evangelicals vote the way they do.

> One 2007 study showed that more than 9 out of 10 evangelicals believe abortion is a major problem—easily making it their top concern. And nearly 8 out of 10 evangelicals say that homosexuality is a major challenge facing the nation. So the fact that many evangelicals are reluctant to describe their voting as primarily focused on these issues seems to reflect their self-awareness rather than their stances on the issues. Like anyone else, many evangelicals care about their image and do not want to be pigeon-holed as one- or two-issue voters, even though these social and moral issues remain very significant for many evangelicals.[48]

45. Mann and Ornstein, *It's Worse than It Looks*, 122.

46. Bean, *The Politics of Evangelical Identity*, 1.

47. Ibid., 18.

48. Kinnaman, "How Americans View 'Evangelical Voters.'"

The results of this particular survey are very significant. They underscore the fact that even though evangelicals in the pew admit to doubts about theological claims they hear preached and taught, their politics remains faithful to the moral agenda that theology promotes. This is why evangelicalism remains the force in Republican politics that it is. *Monolithic* may be too strong a word to describe the evangelical Republican constituency, but solid and reliable are not. This is because theological doubts don't translate into a different way of looking at the world for people who remain connected to evangelical churches. Evangelical moral teachings have a strong hold on people because of the need for certainty in an ever-changing world. Personal doubts cannot compete with words of assurance from clergy who speak in absolutes, who insist they know the will of God and what God wants and does not want.

It was predictable, then, that evangelical responses to Pope Francis issuing a statement saying that priests could absolve women who have had an abortion who are seeking forgiveness would be swift and critical. Gene Veith, Provost of the evangelical Patrick Henry College in Virginia, was quick to condemn the pope's decision as " another example of the Gospel-denying effects of the Roman Catholic penitential system." It is God who pardons sin," Veith declared, "because of Jesus' sacrifice on the cross. No human agent could provide forgiveness including a pope."[49] Russell Moore, who bemoaned evangelical support for Donald Trump, rebuked the pope's declaration as well when he tweeted, "Repentant sinners can be forgiven of any sin, at any time, on the basis of the life and blood of Christ. That's the gospel."[50]

Several years ago Tony Campolo, one of the most prominent evangelicals of the last fifty years, expressed alarm about the political direction evangelicalism was taking:

> What scares me is that [evangelical] Christianity in America today sees nothing wrong with being allied with political conservatism. Conservatives are people who worship at the graves of dead radicals. Stop to think about that. The people who started this country, George Washington, Jefferson, Hamilton, these were not conservatives; these were the radicals of the time. In fact, conservatives always look back on people who they despised and make them into heroes. If you were to listen to the religious right today, they

49. Young, "Why evangelicals are attacking Pope Francis on Abortion."
50. Russell Moore @drmoore.

would make you believe that Martin Luther King was one of their flock. In reality, they hated him and did everything they could to destroy him."[51]

It should come as no surprise that Campolo is considered by many other evangelical leaders as a traitor to the cause, especially since he has come out in support of gay marriage. At best we might say that the evangelical community is divided between those who want evangelicals to take a more compassionate, softer tone on issues of the day and those who believe it is time to double down on absolute positions. *Divide* is probably too strong a word to use, though. It is more of a difference than a divide given the fact that at the moment evangelicals remain the reliable Republican constituency they have been for many years. They seem to fit together like a hand and glove since both want certainty, consider ambiguity a tool of moral relativism, and believe compromise is capitulation. This is why Barry Goldwater did not want the Republican Party to get involved with evangelicals. He knew that in a democratic society ruled by civility political leaders have to understand the efficacy of compromise to advance the causes of freedom and justice for all.

It is evangelical activity and behavior in American political life as a whole and the Republican Party in particular that is my primary concern. Evangelical beliefs matter because they are critical to understanding why evangelicals do what they do. Words can hurt, but when acted upon they do damage that may not be undone. Their beliefs have convinced them that they are doing what is right and also right for the nation. The pages that follow will tell a different story. The place to begin is in comparing the position evangelicals hold in regard to the major moral issue of today with the way most Americans think about those same issues. That is the subject of the next chapter.

51. Falsani, "Why Tony Campolo's LGBTQ Reversal is Evangelicalism's Tipping Point."

2

HOSTAGE TAKING

POLITICAL HOSTAGE TAKING IS an intriguing concept Mann and Ornstein define as "putting political expediency above the national interest and tribal hubris above cooperative problem solving."[1] Equally destructive, "it blocks any attempt to balance interests, have meaningful debate on issues, and nurtures disrespect for opponents."[2] But, they say, political hostage taking is not unique to battles in Congress, but is a "template for all that is wrong with our contemporary society and politics."[3]

It is truly disconcerting to believe Christians would be of such a mind-set that what they are doing is comparable to political hostage taking, but the attitude evangelicals display on moral issues seems to warrant the comparison. They show no concern for national interests except to believe their views will save America from moral corruption. Their intransigence suggests a basic hubris that insists their way is the only way. And the certainty with which they hold convictions has helped push the Republicans in Congress to do precisely what Mann and Ornstein say happens in political hostage taking—no desire for meaningful debate, balancing interests, or showing respect for those who disagree with them.

This is why the fact that they are a significant constituency for the Republican Party leads to the conclusion that their collective presence in American politics is hurting rather than helping the country. Let me be clear about what is at stake here. The decline I am talking about is in regard to our political process, not America itself. Evangelicals often speak about the moral decline of America, but the evidence does not in any way support

1. Mann and Ornstien, *It's Even Worse than It Looks,* 4.
2. Ibid., 26.
3. Ibid.

their claim. If the moral fiber of our nation is at risk it is only because it always has been and always will be. It's the nature of civic life. Rather than our public morality declining, I submit it is better than it once was. Americans tend to romanticize our history as if those who founded this nation were sensitive to truth and justice more than we are today.

But the US Constitution itself proves otherwise, given the fact that our founders who wrote it owned slaves, and never understood the evil it represented, so that "liberty and justice for all" was a phrase that intended to speak for white citizens and no one else. Moreover, the Old West was nothing like the movies we saw growing up with heroes we wanted to be like. It was, instead, a place where drunks, rapists, cattle rustlers, outlaws, and gunslingers made everyone else fear for their lives. And most of the people who talk about "taking their country back" are probably thinking about the 1950s, when white supremacy ruled, women had no rights, and no families looked or lived like the Cleavers on *Leave It To Beaver*.

More true than anything about Americans today is that we are as good and as imperfect as we ever were. We have made progress on some fronts while perpetuating bad things on the other. Slavery and segregation are gone, but racism and discrimination are still present. Workers are treated better and paid more than they once were, but corporations still exploit them and throw them away like trash when it serves their bottom line. I could go on, but the point is that talk of the moral decline of America is a straw wall evangelical preachers love to knock down as they lead the charge to promote an agenda that would take us back to old days that were hardly as "good" as they have been made out to be.

In thinking about the role of evangelicalism in politics it is essential to identify the end to which they are trying to push the nation. In light of the majority views of Americans on every major social and moral issue we face, it is clear that evangelicalism does not represent where most people are. On the contrary, as James Davison Hunter pointed out twenty-five years ago, most Americans do not embrace any particular moral vision wholly or uncritically.[4] One way evangelicals have reacted to this reality is by promoting the myth of America in moral crisis. In addition, their voting power in the Republican Party has led to the election of Senators and Representatives who have adopted the same *no compromise* attitude evangelicals have when it comes to theology. At this point evangelicals have not succeeded in imposing their will on the nation as a whole, but they have contributed to

4. Hunter, *Cultural Wars*, 45.

our political system reaching a stalemate. Unreasonable demands coupled with an uncompromising attitude always leads to dysfunction, chaos, and usually deep divisions that take generations to heal.

In some ways it is understandable how this has happened. Moral decisions are never simple, but when a group of people believe they are, unthinking and sometimes unhinged individuals go to extremes in the name of God. Evangelicals know only the colors white and black, refusing to acknowledge the reality that public morality always has a social context and that context affects the way we see right and wrong, truth and lies, as they are applied to actual circumstances. How many relationships have been damaged, how many people have been hurt, how many injustices have been justified, all by people who sincerely believed they were right in their thinking and doing what was right turned out to be very wrong. A father rejects his daughter because she is in love with another woman and loses her to what would have been forever until he discovers he has a terminal illness. The mother calls her daughter and tells her about her father. She comes home to see him and they reconcile. He dies with her by his side, both of them feeling the sadness over all the years of being together they missed because he thought he was right.

An important part of the social context in which morality exists is its legal implications. "The law," as theologian Stanley Hauerwas has observed, "is our way of negotiating safe agreements between autonomous individuals who have nothing else in common other than their fear of death and their mutual desire for protection."[5] When evangelicals made the choice to become politically partisan, the locus of their work moved from sanctuaries to Congress, but it seems as if they failed to anticipate the diversity of people and views they would encounter. Consensus on the specifics of public morality is far more difficult to achieve in culture than in a congregation of like-minded people whose only goal is to be Christian. America is not a church and not all Americans are Christians. Laws cannot run roughshod over this fact and be ruled constitutional. Negotiating between moral convictions and laws requires a willingness to see both sides, weighing opposing opinions, and in the end reaching a compromise that first and foremost satisfies constitutional requirements, with the hope that the compromise in some way promotes public morality.

The extent to which evangelicals ignore this need for compromise in making laws is what is contributing to the decline of the American political

---

5. Hauerwas, "Abortion Theologically Understood."

process. Their attitude and actions give the strong impression that they would prefer to live in a theocracy of their own choosing than to accept the give-and-take required of citizens of a democracy. As this discussion continues the picture that will emerge is one that shows the contrast between rigidity and intransigency and the need for flexibility and humility.

EVANGELICALS AND SAME-SEX MARRIAGE

Prior to the 2015 Supreme Court ruling that legalized gay marriage across the country, we had a donnybrook here in Minnesota over this issue. It was in so many ways a sad example of the refusal of evangelicals to accept that the law is our nation's "way of negotiating safe agreements between autonomous individuals who have nothing else in common other than their fear of death and their mutual desire for protection."

Amending the Minnesota state constitution is easier than it is in many states, requiring only a simple majority in both the House and Senate to put an amendment on the ballot without needing the governor's signature. Once evangelical churches and the Archdiocese of Minneapolis/St. Paul threw their full weight behind the proposed anti-gay marriage amendment, its passage seemed all but certain. I was asked to participate in a debate on the proposed amendment at one of our local high schools. A member of the state House of Representatives and I debated a member of the state Senate and the senior minister of a large evangelical church in the area.

The typical arguments favoring the amendment were presented by the opposition, ranging from the nature of marriage being for procreation to the Bible speaking of marriage as being between a man and a woman only. Implicit in their arguments was, of course, their view that the Bible openly condemns homosexuality itself as a sin. My partner and I countered with our own arguments: (1) that the Bible was not a very helpful guide to marriage since polygamy was widely practiced in ancient Israel; (2) that Torah law not only allowed for divorce, but did so in a way that confirmed the "property" status of women that existed even at the time of Jesus, making his teaching on divorce a direct challenge to Torah law on divorce; (3) that if marriage was solely for procreation, childless couples should be forced to get divorced; (4) that the belief that sex is only for procreation goes back to a time when that applied only to women because men were free to enjoy recreational sex at their own discretion and pleasure; (5) that legal marriage is a right enjoyed by all citizens, not some, and that laws against same-sex marriage represent a violation of the civil rights of gay and lesbians who are just as American as heterosexuals.

In the end the overwhelming majority of the students said in the poll taken after the debate that they found the arguments for the amendment unconvincing. So did the entire state. Most outside observers thought Minnesota would be the thirty-second state to pass such a measure, keeping the streak of thirty-one wins and no losses for anti-gay marriage states alive. They were wrong. The amendment was defeated by a large margin. What is more, Republicans lost control of the legislature. With complete control of both houses and the governor's office a year later Democrats repealed the anti-gay marriage law that had already been on the books when the amendment was pushed by the religious community.

Minnesotans showed that voters understand when there is overreach on moral issues. With an anti–same-sex marriage law already on the books, wanting to change the state constitution was widely seen as extreme and was rejected. A constitutional change was taking this battle to a very different level to which Minnesota voters did not want to go. This vote also underscored the belief I think most Americans have that reasonable people should be able to find reasonable ways to compromise in the face of disagreement, especially when moral beliefs and the law of the land are in conflict. This is why polls show that they agreed with Justice Anthony Kennedy's statements for the majority when he wrote in the Court's same-sex marriage decision in 2015, "No longer may this liberty be denied. No union is more profound than marriage, for it embodies the highest ideals of love, fidelity, devotion, sacrifice and family. In forming a marital union, two people become something greater than once they were." He acknowledged further that marriage is a "keystone of our social order" and that all the plaintiffs in the case were seeking was "equal dignity in the eyes of the law."[6]

Unfortunately evangelicals have refused to see the value of this attitude on moral issues, instead being angered by the Supreme Court ruling enough to dare to defy it. In Alabama Chief Supreme Court Justice Roy Moore, an ardent evangelical judge, ignored his colleagues and issued an administrative order telling probate judges throughout the state to ignore the Supreme Court by refusing to issue licenses to same-sex couples. "Until further decision by the Alabama Supreme Court," the Moore order said, "the existing orders . . . that Alabama probate judges have a ministerial duty not to issue any marriage license contrary to the Alabama Sanctity of

6. Kennedy, *Obergefell et al.*

Marriage Amendment or the Alabama Marriage Protection Act remain in full force and effect."[7]

Federal prosecutors in Alabama reacted swiftly to Moore, issuing a strong rebuttal of his actions:

> The Chief Justice of the Alabama Supreme Court has issued an administrative order, directing probate judges that they may not issue marriage licenses to same-sex couples, despite the U.S. Supreme Court's decision last year on marriage equality. We have grave concerns about this order, which directs Alabama probate judges to disobey the ruling of the Supreme Court," said U.S. Attorneys Joyce White Vance of the Northern District of Alabama and Kenyen Brown of the Southern District of Alabama. Government officials are free to disagree with the law, but not to disobey it. This issue has been decided by the highest court in the land and Alabama must follow that law.[8]

The Alabama Supreme Court also reacted when the remaining members rejected a petition by the Alabama Policy Institute, the Alabama Citizens Action Program, and a county probate judge to officially declare that the state's prohibition on gay marriage still stood in defiance of the US Supreme Court. In May of 2016 the Alabama Judicial Inquiry Commission went a step further and forwarded charges to the Alabama Court of the Judiciary accusing Moore of actions that violated judicial ethics. He was suspended pending the outcome of his trial.

Moore is being represented by the evangelical legal organization Liberty Counsel, founded by Matthew Staver, who was once dean of the online law school of Liberty University. Staver and his group also counseled Kim Davis, clerk of Rowan County, Kentucky, to defy the Supreme Court ruling and refuse to issue marriage licenses to gay couples after US District Court Judge David Bunning ordered her to do so. That landed her in jail for a brief period. Judge Bunning released her with instructions not to interfere with the deputy clerks who were issuing licenses to all couples. Staver continued to use one legal maneuver after another to keep the fight going, finally appealing Bunning's decision to the Sixth Circuit Court of Appeals in Cincinnati, arguing that Davis was a "prisoner of conscience" who could not do her job and follow her conscience. Allowing her to follow her conscience,

7. Cason, "Roy Moore says probate judges have duty to enforce same-sex marriage ban."

8. Domonoske, "Alabama Chief Justice Orders Judges To Enforce Ban On Same-Sex Marriage."

he insisted, would not place an undue burden on gay couples since they could easily go to the clerk's office in another county.

It is curious that opponents of same-sex marriage have created a mythical history of marriage that does not hold up under scrutiny. Contrasting the notion that marriage is an act sanctioned by God wherein a man and a woman declare a covenant of eternal and everlasting love, marriage had a utilitarian purpose. It was considered "a way of getting in-laws, of making alliances and expanding the family labor force."[9] Then, of course, there were arranged marriages, more common than many Americans realize. Its widespread practice makes it difficult not to think that the way evangelicals talk about "traditional" marriage is actually made-up history that ignores the fact that it has always been a ritual with different meanings in different cultures. If in our culture marriage is believed to be holy, it is because it is an expression of faithful love, enduring love, hard-working love, love that people of faith believe is of God. But that holiness does not depend on sexual orientation, the color of one's skin, nationality, religious beliefs, or other extraneous characteristics. Love is universal and does not know or is limited by artificial barriers we humans erect to undermine it.

That is why we have managed along the way to do terrible things in the name of love and God. One of the most heartwrenching stories of such a terrible thing was the marriage of Mildred Jeter and Richard Loving whose only "sin" was being of different races. *Loving v. Virginia* was cited in the 2015 Supreme Court argument in favor of gay marriage, and for good reason.

In 1958 a Virginia couple, Mildred Jeter, who was black, and Richard Loving, who was white, drove into the District of Columbia, got married, and then returned to Caroline County not far from my hometown to begin their life together. In the fall after their June wedding charges were brought against them that their marriage violated a Virginia law banning interracial marriage. They pleaded guilty and were sentenced to a year in jail. But the Caroline County Circuit Court judge said he would suspend their sentence for a period of twenty-five years if they agreed to move out of Virginia and not return for a commensurate period of time. In his decision the judge wrote: "Almighty God created the races white, black, yellow, malay and red, and he placed them on separate continents. And, but for the interference with his arrangement, there would be no cause for such marriage. The fact

9. Coontz, *Marriage, a History.*

that he separated the races shows that he did not intend for the races to mix."[10]

The Lovings moved to DC, where they filed a motion in the state trial court to vacate the judgment and set aside the sentence on the grounds that the statutes they had violated were superseded by their Fourteenth Amendment rights as American citizens. For two years they filed one appeal after another, but each time the courts refused to set aside their conviction or nullify the Virginia anti-miscegenation statute, the state Supreme Court of Appeals declaring that the state's legitimate purposes were "to preserve the racial integrity of its citizens," and to prevent "the corruption of blood," "a mongrel breed of citizens," and "the obliteration of racial pride." In short, the Court of Appeals endorsed the doctrine of white supremacy and then applied it to include the state's right to protect marriage.[11]

The Lovings appealed the decision to the US Supreme Court that chose to hear the case. Arguments were heard in April of 1967, and on June 12 the Supreme Court ruled the Virginia anti-miscegenation law prohibiting interracial marriage was unconstitutional, and the Lovings later returned to their home in Virginia where they had three children and lived the remainder of their lives.

Predictably, the *Loving v. Virginia* case was cited in the 2015 Supreme Court case that changed the landscape of marriage across the country. *Loving v. Virginia* had already exposed the misuse of the Bible to justify marital discrimination on the basis of race. In making reference to it, the Supreme Court was implicitly exposing the same misuse by those seeking to justify marital discrimination on the basis of sexual orientation. Moreover, since the state judge who first convicted the Lovings justified his decision on his personal belief that God did not intend for the races to mix and certainly not to marry, rather than the Constitution, both rulings underscored the distinction courts must make between religious convictions and the rule of law.

That distinction is not a difficult concept to understand for any open-minded person. My ninety-eight-year-old mother proved this to me. As you might expect, my mother is of a generation that has trouble not only accepting gay marriage, but understanding it. Thus, she says she does not believe in same-sex marriage. She also knows that I do. Four years ago my wife and I were visiting her a couple of weeks after the state of North

10. *Loving v. Virginia.*

11. Ibid.

Carolina, where she lives, held a vote on an anti-gay marriage initiative. As you might also expect, it passed by an overwhelming margin. One night at the dinner table I brought up the gay marriage ban just to have some fun with her. "So, Mother," I asked with a sly smile on my face, "how did you vote on the anti-gay marriage initiative a few weeks ago?" Of course, I already knew the answer to my question, that is, until she shocked all of us when she replied, "I voted against it." Taken aback, I responded, "You voted against it? Why did you do that? You don't believe in gay marriage." Without missing a beat she said, "I know I don't, but I don't think I should be able to tell somebody else who they can marry."

Since that night I have thought many, many times about how much better our nation and certainly our politics would be if all evangelicals could see the integrity and wisdom in what my mother said. She understood very well that she could hold on to what she believed without imposing her personal beliefs on everyone else. My mother wants everyone to be a Christian. She wants everyone to go to heaven. She wants love to be the strongest force in the world. But she knows none of that can be imposed on anyone. She knows that when Scripture instructs her to be willing to give an account of the hope that is within her, it also says to do so with "gentleness and reverence" (1 Pet 3:15). And my very gentle and very wise mother knows most of all that forcing your own moral views on everyone else is not the way American democracy works.

This says to me that the issue for evangelicals is not whether to hold firm to their moral principles when it comes to gay marriage (or any other moral conviction that has public consequences), but *how* to hold on to them. The Supreme Court decision on gay marriage invited the nation to understand that collective rights apply to all Americans or to none, and that denying the legitimacy of love between same-sex couples is a greater threat to the sanctity of marriage than affirming it. The fact that surveys show clearly that evangelicals reject this balanced approach is why they are part of the problem instead of part of the solution.

EVANGELICALS AND HOMOSEXUALITY

Post-Baby Boomer generations have a much more accepting attitude toward homosexuals and transgender individuals because they have many friends who are out. Their experience is the opposite of what Boomers experienced in an age where homosexuality was widely believed to be a mental disease. That was when homosexuals kept their sexual orientation a secret because of the scorn and threat to their safety should anyone find out. Often gays and lesbians would move to New York, San Francisco, and other major cities once they reached adulthood, to be with others whose sexual orientation was like their own. It was not until the late '70s that the American Psychiatric Association removed homosexuality from the category of mental disorder. In the minds of too many then and now homosexuality is associated with pedophilia, showing a fundamental ignorance of both.

The progress that has been made in understanding homosexuality and in the way gays and lesbians are treated shows that most Americans have been willing to learn and grow. The stunning turnabout in attitude about same-sex marriage in a few short years proves that human beings can change. Evangelicals, on the other hand, have chosen, instead, to live in the past as if we have learned nothing about sexual orientation. It is their insistence that homosexuality is a sin that is the fundamental reason for their homophobic attitude. They meet the very definition of the word: "an irrational fear of, aversion to, or discrimination against homosexuality or homosexuals." The key word is "fear." People usually hate anything they don't understand, and the root of that hate is fear, which is the opposite of love according to the Bible itself (1 John 4:18). What makes fear of homosexuality sinister and powerful is that evangelicals don't want to admit they are in its grip. Thus, they fall back on an unwarranted certainty about what they believe that in their own mind releases them from the responsibility for being wrong.

Yet there are some evangelical leaders who are suggesting the Bible may not be the last word on the subject. Evangelical Peter Wehner said in a 2013 article for Patheos:

> Precisely where one lands on the matter of the appropriate societal stance toward homosexuality and same sex marriage isn't dependent on Biblical literacy. Faithful Christians can hold different views on when and how to apply a Biblical view on a range of sexual matters, as well as the spirit that animates their position.
>
> What I think this comes down to, as so many things in life come down to, is discretion, prudence, and wisdom. Some of us are drawn to certain issues and rhetoric that we believe honor the righteousness of God; others of us are drawn to certain issues and rhetoric that we believe honor the grace of God. Would Jesus, if He were here today, be speaking out against gays and their political agenda based on what might be called a theological anthropology?

Or would He be more inclined to warn critics of homosexuality against stridency, judgmentalism and blindness to many other matters (like acquisitiveness) that we so easily ignore? Or would He be challenging everyone, in different ways, based on their particular challenges and needs and the state of their hearts?[12]

He then adds a very revealing hopeful conclusion: "None of us can know for sure. We all see through a glass darkly."[13]

As hopeful as Wehner's comments are, nothing points to his view gaining wide acceptance among evangelicals. In a 2015 survey more than 60 percent of mainline Christians and 70 percent of Catholics said they believed homosexuality should be accepted by society, but the same survey found that only 36 percent of evangelicals did.[14] What is more, when Tony Campolo stated publicly that he no longer believed homosexuality was a sin and that he now supports gay marriage, a position his wife has held for more than two decades, he was resoundingly criticized for being misguided and guilty of listening to his wife and his gay friends instead of the Bible. Denny Burk, Professor of Biblical Studies at Boyce College, wrote on his blog, "Like many others before him, Campolo's conscience seems to have been moved not by scripture but by relationships he's had with gay friends."[15]

Albert Mohler, President of Southern Baptist Theological Seminary, believes people like Campolo are a sign that evangelicals are headed for a split. "This issue will eventually break relationships: personally, congregationally and institutionally. There's not going to be any way around it."[16] Another comment found on an evangelical website was even more direct:

> Tony Campolo recently said this about gay-marriage, "(L)ike so many other Christians, I was deeply uncertain about what was right." But the Bible is crystal clear on sexual sin, including homosexuality. Unfortunately, those who are sounding the alarm are often categorized as irrational, judgmental, bigoted and intolerant. But how can we warn if we won't confront, correct if we won't

12. Wehner, "An Evangelical Christian Looks at Homosexuality."

13. Ibid.

14. Murphey, "Most U.S. Christian groups grow more accepting of homosexuality."

15. Burk, " Three Observations about Tony Campolo's acceptance of committed gay relationships."

16. Bailey, "From Franklin Graham to Tony Campolo."

challenge and contend if we won't question? We must speak the truth in love. Opinions change, but truth does not.[17]

The confidence with which Mohler speaks of a coming split itself suggests there is little room for a moderation of views on homosexuality among evangelicals. As Mohler said adamantly in response to a book by Matthew Vines, an evangelical Harvard graduate who describes his personal experience of coming out and insists the Bible does not condemn homosexuality,[18] "Contrary to Vines' pleas on behalf of people who want to be true to their sexual orientation and to their faith, that one can be gay or Christian, but not both."[19]

. Mohler's comments are typical of what most evangelicals believe. They put no stock in scientific research that has found genetics plays a decisive role in sexual orientation, otherwise they would stop insisting that gays and lesbians have chosen to be the way they are and can "un-choose" if they want to. At this point research affirms that both nature and nurture play a role in sexual orientation, but even the latter consists of factors beyond a person's control, things like early nutrition, poverty, a mother's love, even exposure to toxic chemicals.[20] Former director of the National Institutes of Health, Dr. Francis S. Collins, a self-avowed evangelical, says it has been established as a scientific fact that there is a genetic persuasion in regard to sexual orientation.

> The evidence we have at present strongly supports the proposition that there are hereditary factors in male homosexuality— he observation that an identical twin of a male homosexual has approximately a 20% likelihood of also being gay points to this conclusion, since that is 10 times the population incidence. But the fact that the answer is not 100% also suggests that other factors besides DNA must be involved. That certainly doesn't imply, however, that those other undefined factors are inherently alterable.[21]

---

17. Idelman, "5 Ways Tony Campolo and Others Miss the Bible Mark With New Views on Gay Christians."

18. Vines, *God and the Gay Christian*.

19. Ford, "How A New Book About Gay Christians Is Reviving Evangelical Homophobia."

20. Healym, "Scientists find DNA differences between gay men and their straight twin brothers."

21. Throckmorton, "Dr. Francis Collins comments on homosexuality and genetics." .

In other words, sexual orientation is not solely a matter of choice for anyone. I did not choose to be attracted to my wife. Our lesbian friends did not choose to be attracted to each other. In both instances many factors played a role, almost all of them unconscious and beyond the realm of choice. Yet these facts are treated as speculation, theory, or mere opinion by evangelicals whose minds are already closed.

This is what makes the absoluteness of the evangelical conviction that homosexuality is a sin seem not only judgmental, but arbitrary. They have every right to believe as they do, but they are not content to leave it at that. They want to place moral sanctions on gays and lesbians from enjoying the same rights of citizenship that they have. As I have already pointed out, marriage is a civil institution with religious meaning only when it takes place in a church. The freedom of ministers and churches not to perform gay weddings is not and has not been in jeopardy, although evangelicals want people to believe it is. The fact is, I can refuse to do a wedding for anyone for any reason with impunity. It is solely my decision, just as Catholic priests often refuse to participate in a Protestant/Catholic wedding if the couple does not pledge to be Catholic.

It is taking their beliefs beyond reasonable limits when evangelicals try to prevent same-sex couples the civil right to marry. Churches and clergy are not required to host gay weddings. That freedom is sufficient to allow evangelicals to stay true to what they believe without insisting that no church and no clergy can host a wedding or perform a ceremony. That most Americans saw evangelical anti-gay marriage campaigns for what they were and have welcomed the Supreme Court decision speaks well of our nation. There has never been any political or constitutional basis for evangelical efforts to prevent gay marriage, which leaves religious beliefs as the only explanation for their past actions and continued attitude, another example of why it is important to connect the dots between evangelical and right-wing Republicans politics.

EVANGELICALS AND SAME-SEX ADOPTION

Same-sex married couples have been able to adopt children in Illinois since 1995, but three religious agencies, Catholic Charities, Lutheran Child and Family Services of Illinois (LCFS), and the Evangelical Child and Family Agency, refuse to allow it. It does not matter how qualified a same-sex couple may be to parent a child, these agencies reject them. They are not discriminating against gay couples, they say, just exercising their freedom to practice what they believe. But their actions are rooted in the same misguided view of homosexuality that evangelicals use to justify their rejection of same-sex marriage.

Part of the frustration in confronting these discriminatory actions is the material fed to them by groups such as the Family Research Council (FRC) that is bogus "science." Currently, for example, the FRC has a propaganda article posted on its website entitled "Ten Arguments From Social Science Against Same-Sex Marriage." Not one of them does what the article claims. They are, instead, general social principles that do not speak directly about same-sex marriage at all. The following is a quote from the book *Growing Up with a Single Parent: What Hurts, What Helps,* by Sara McLanahan and Gary Sandefur, which they claim speaks against same-sex marriage when it is actually about why two-parent families are preferable to single parenting.

> If we were asked to design a system for making sure that children's basic needs were met, we would probably come up with something quite similar to the two-parent ideal. Such a design, in theory, would not only ensure that children had access to the time and money of two adults, it also would provide a system of checks and balances that promoted quality parenting. The fact that both parents have a biological connection to the child would increase the likelihood that the parents would identify with the child and be willing to sacrifice for that child, and it would reduce the likelihood that either parent would abuse the child.[22]

Acknowledging that the traditional nuclear family model is the ideal is not the same thing as arguing against same-sex marriage or adoption. So when the FRC claims that "a large and growing body of scientific evidence indicates that the intact, married family is best for children," therefore same-sex marriage and adoption is harmful or wrong, it is distorting the truth.

It is difficult to know how to respond to this kind of intellectual dishonesty. But one way may be to cite empirical evidence that demonstrates the fallacy of evangelical arguments. I am thinking of seven children of four different same-sex couples I have known over the last fifteen years. Three of them were infants when they came to our church and are now between the ages of seven and ten. One was four and is now in high school. Another one

22. McLanahan and Sandefur, *Growing Up with a Single Parent,* 38.

was six and is now seventeen. These children are as well adjusted as other kids. The two teenagers are doing well in school, in sports, and in life. The younger ones are a delight to be around. All of the parents are adults anyone would enjoy knowing and would feel blessed to count as friends. Four are the biological children of one of the mothers in each of three couples. Three children are adopted. There seems to be no difference in the degree to which they are well adjusted for their ages whether they are natural born or adopted.

These families are what we all want for ourselves—good families. They live the way most other families lives. The parents work and the children go to school, have sleepovers, play sports, vacation together, visit grandparents, and get into trouble like all kids do. It is a disservice to them, but also to all families and to our nation, to ignore the fact that sexual orientation has no bearing on the ability of men and women to be good parents. Rather, it is the content of their personal character that matters, and as Dr. King said, that is how they should be judged.

EVANGELICALISM AND ABORTION

Put yourself in this situation. Your college-age daughter is walking back to campus one night after waitressing at a nearby restaurant when she is accosted by a man who pulls her behind large shrubs and rapes her. Thankfully he doesn't kill her. When she regains her senses she immediately goes to the campus security office and reports what happened. They call the city police and the police call you. Luckily you live in a town not far from where your daughter goes to college. You are there as quickly as possible, walk into the room, and see her bruised face, her torn clothes, and dried tears on her cheeks. You go to her side and pull her into your arms and whisper, "You will get through this, sweetheart. Your father and I will be with you every step of the way."

Weeks later you are with your daughter when the doctor tells her she is pregnant. She immediately declares that she will never have her rapist's baby. But she has no choice. Abortion in America is illegal. She will have to carry the pregnancy to full term, then face the decision to either keep the baby or give him/her up for adoption. But there is another choice. Abortion is legal in some countries in Europe and you have the money to take her there to have one. As it turns out, your daughter has a choice after all because you have the financial means to make that choice possible. It's her decision and you support it because you agree that no woman who is raped should be forced to have the baby of the rapist.

This story may well have been the story of all raped women before 1973 here in America. In fact, it was the story of any and every woman who had an unwanted pregnancy. Take Sherri Finkbine, a television star who hosted *Romper Room* in the early '60s. Early in her pregnancy she had taken thalidomide that was being prescribed for morning sickness. Then doctors discovered that it caused severe birth defects. Sherri Finkbine was told there were signs that her pregnancy had been compromised by the drug. She made the decision to abort and arranged to have it done at a large hospital in Phoenix. Before the procedure was done, however, she told her story to a reporter to warn other pregnant women of the dangers of thalidomide. Her plans to have an abortion caused such an uproar that the hospital pulled out and the doctor refused to do the procedure. With no alternative here in the States, she ended up traveling to Sweden, where abortion was legal.

This is the world evangelicals want our nation to go back to, where choice is not an option and certainly not for women with no financial resources. Before *Roe v. Wade* a few states allowed abortion in the case of rape or incest, but most didn't. A couple of states also allowed it when the woman's life was in danger, but few doctors anywhere in the country would do abortions. Evangelicals believe this America was superior to the America we live in now because they believe abortion is sinful, an act of murder. The circumstances don't matter because they believe nothing in life happens unless God allows it. They are sure they speak for the unborn as if the mother does not care what happens.

In May of 2016 the Oklahoma legislature passed an evangelical-sponsored bill that would make anyone who performs or induces an abortion guilty of committing a felony subject to serving one to three years in the state penitentiary. State Senator Nathan Dahm, who sponsored the bill, said that he believed life begins at conception, precisely the belief *Roe v. Wade* acknowledged was one view, but not the only one and not one supported by medical fact. Dham knew that, but still wanted to create the need for the Supreme Court to review that decision and overturn it.[23] Not surprisingly Liberty Counsel helped write the bill and had pledged to defend it in court, but the governor chose to veto it to avoid that inevitable scenario.

23. Berman, "Oklahoma legislature passes bill making it a felony to perform abortions."

Despite what evangelicals want to believe, though, moral principles become real only when they are applied to real-life situations, but those situations affect the way principles are applied. If we were talking about how churches deal with abortion the issue would not be nearly as complicated. Stanley Hauerwas says the question would not be what the woman should do. It would be what the congregation would do. It would be as much their decisions as hers because she would know they are in this thing together. Hauerwas believes that both the pro-life and pro-choice sides on this issue are asking the wrong questions because for Christians the issue is not one of rights. It is "a reminder about the kind of community that we need to be. Abortion language reminds the church to be ready to receive new life as church."[24] While Hauerwas's view is provocative and perhaps corrective in the way Christians think about this issue, abortion is not just a church issue or a Christian issue. It is an American issue involving more than Christians and more than a sectarian morality. Diverse views about abortion have pushed this issue out of the church and into the courts as a way of finding some balance between what is moral and what is legal.

Read with an open mind it is obvious that the 1973 *Roe v. Wade* Supreme Court decision was an effort to find a "safe agreement" about abortion. If you read the ruling you see that the seven justices who voted in favor of it and the two who objected were trying to make an honest attempt to achieve a balance between morality and legality. Writing for the majority, Justice Harry Blackmun explained:

> We forthwith acknowledge our awareness of the sensitive and emotional nature of the abortion controversy, of the vigorous opposing views, even among physicians, and of the deep and seemingly absolute convictions that the subject inspires. One's philosophy, one's experiences, one's exposure to the raw edges of human existence, one's religious training, one's attitudes toward life and family and their values, and the moral standards one establishes and seeks to observe, are all likely to influence and to color one's thinking and conclusions about abortion.[25]

This decision was also intended to bring clarity to very uneven practices on abortion rights across the nation. Before 1973 states had different laws on abortion, and a few had no laws at all. In 1969 Norma McCorvey ("Jane Roe") filed a lawsuit claiming that a Texas law criminalizing all

24. Hauerwas, "Abortion, Theologically Understood."
25. United States Supreme Court, *Roe v. Wade.*

abortions except when the woman's life was in jeopardy violated her constitutional rights. While two other parties filed similar suits against Texas at the same time, the Court rejected hearing them and focused exclusively on Jane Roe's. The Court also agreed to hear the case of *Doe v. Bolton* that challenged abortion laws in the state of Georgia. While the court ruled in favor of the plaintiff in that case and overturned Georgia's abortion restrictions as well, the *Roe v. Wade* ruling became the focus of the public's attention on the subject and has been the point of debate ever since.

The Supreme Court decision did not declare that a woman had an unrestricted right to choose an abortion, as some evangelicals assert, nor did it affirm the state's freedom to pass laws that ignore a woman's right to privacy. Instead, it ruled that the Texas law was based on the view that life begins at conception, a belief the Court said could be true, but was not an established medical fact. This belief that life begins at conception, the Court ruled, led Texas to enact a law that was too broad and too general to meet constitutional demands, especially in regard to the Fourteenth Amendment that forbids the state from depriving any person of life, liberty, or property without due process of law.

Overturning the Texas law, the Court went on to say, did not mean that the state had no "compelling interests" in the well-being of the fetus regardless of when life begins, only that such interests could not abridge a woman's Fourteenth Amendment rights. Thus, it declared: "The right of personal privacy includes the abortion decision, but that this right is not unqualified, and must be considered against important state interests in regulation." In other words, the Court's decision overturned the Texas law prohibiting abortion and also declared that the Fourteenth Amendment protected Jane Roe's right to terminate her pregnancy. But it also said that this right was limited to the first trimester. Thereafter, the state's "compelling interests" in the welfare of the woman and the fetus could be a basis for placing reasonable limits on choice. Further, the Court said that if Texas (or any state) did impose such limits, it would have to show why those specific limits met the standard of "compelling interests" in protecting both the mother and the fetus.

In his dissent from the majority's decision, Justice Byron White did not address the issue of abortion itself, but focused on the Court's use, or in his opinion, misuse, of the Fourteenth Amendment as a basis for ruling that choice was a woman's constitutional right. In short, White did not believe freedom of choice regarding abortion was guaranteed by the Constitution. Whether he believed choice was right or wrong did not matter. What he rejected was the argument by the Court's majority that the Constitution assured a woman of that right, arguing that it should be left to the discretion of the legislative process. Conservatives on the Court have consistently agreed with Justice White ever since.

Even with the controversy that has followed that decision surveys show that the majority of Americans believe it was the right one. More than 90 percent believe abortion should be legal in all or most circumstances.[26] Like the justices voting in the majority in *Roe v. Wade* they do not believe abortion should be without restrictions, only that in principle they support a woman's right to choose. They are not unaware of the desire of abortion opponents to speak for the unborn, but they are equally aware that the voice of the woman who is pregnant should not be silenced. In truth most Americans are amazingly balanced in their attitude toward abortion rights. Even those who would not make it a choice for themselves still believe it is one they should have the right to make.[27] Perhaps most surprising is to find out that 70 percent of the women who choose abortion self-identify as "Christian," and 23 percent as evangelical. In addition, more than one-third say they attend church once a month, some every week, but all of them choose not to share their decision with other church members out of fear of being the object of gossip.[28]

Americans are not ignoring moral concerns in supporting the right of a woman to make a decision about her own body. They simply believe that in secular society moral beliefs have to be balanced by constitutional rights. For them compromise is the necessary way to find a solution. When former President Bill Clinton said that abortion should be legal, safe, and rare, he spoke for the majority of Americans.

Once again, evangelicals will have none of this. As a way to circumvent *Roe v. Wade* they have devised Targeted Regulation of Abortion Providers (TRAP) laws that restrict abortion access. Twenty-seven states controlled by Republicans have enacted TRAP laws that have placed onerous requirements on abortion clinics, such as: (1) meeting the same standards as ambulatory surgical centers, usually forcing facility renovations clinics cannot afford; (2) requiring clinic doctors who perform abortions to have admitting privileges at nearby hospitals that usually refuse to grant such privileges; (3) requiring a woman to wait twenty-four to forty-eight hours

26. Lipka, "5 facts about abortion."

27. Ibid.

28. Einenkel, "Survey Finds That Christians Have the Most Abortions in U.S."

after an examination before she can have an abortion to make sure she understands what she is doing, sometimes forcing women to travel long distances twice; (4) forcing a woman to have an ultrasound of her pregnancy and even requiring her to view it.

Justification for TRAP laws is said to be a concern for women' safety, but the American College of Obstetricians and Gynecologists, the American Public Health Association, and the American Medical Association have all issued public statements rejecting the need for any of these regulations and insisting that abortion procedures in this country are already safe. But their own statements reveal what evangelicals are truly up to with TRAP laws. When the state of Mississippi passed a TRAP law in 2012, Republican Governor Phil Bryant confirmed the true motivation behind its passage when he said, "Today you see the first step in a movement to do what we campaigned on . . . to try to end abortion in Mississippi."[29] Lieutenant Governor Tate Reeves echoed what Bryant said: "This is a strong bill that will effectively end abortion in Mississippi."[30] All the while the sponsor of the bill, Republican Sam Mims, was insisting, "We believe wholeheartedly that this is a health issue for women."[31]

Efforts to undo *Roe v. Wade* are not likely to go away, although states with TRAP laws were dealt a major setback when in 2016 the Supreme Court ruled against a Texas law that required abortion doctors to have hospital admitting privileges and all abortions to be performed in a hospital-like surgical facility. This case will be discussed in detail in chapter 6. The point here is that each time a state legislature passes a TRAP law, it is almost always because of evangelicals working behind the scene to persuade lawmakers to do so. The nation could be spared these conflicts if evangelicals would accept the fact that after more than thirty years the country has spoken, not in support of immorality, but on behalf of balancing personal freedom with moral principles.

EVANGELICALS AND STEM CELL RESEARCH

Evangelical beliefs about abortion also influence how they think about the relatively new field of stem cell medical research. It was not until 1971 that scientists discovered stem cells in mice. Since then there has been a growing

29. Trinko, "Will Mississippi's last abortion clinic close?"
30. Ibid.
31. Ibid.

body of research and knowledge in this area that holds promise of leading to significant strides in treating diseases and even the potential for rejuvenation of body parts. The subject is more than a little complicated because of the variety of stem cells, but the most promising research centers on early-stage human embryos that are termed human embryonic stem cells (ES cells). These are the ones that have the greatest potential for therapeutic use because they appear to replicate indefinitely and are genetically normal. Scientists believe they will lead to treatment of a variety of diseases such as Type I diabetes, Parkinson's disease, hepatitis, muscular dystrophy, and various forms of cancer. These cells last only about a day before they evolve into other types of cells.

Another cell line is called embryonic germ cells (EG cells) that are harvested from human fetal tissue that may form the three germ layers that make up all the organs of the body. The problem is that they are more developed than ES cells and, thus, are more limited in their potential use. But both are flash points for the current controversy over stem cell research. Evangelical and Catholic leaders together oppose the use of ES cells because it involves the destruction of the embryo.

In March of 2005 the National Association of Evangelicals (NAE) tried to speak for the evangelical community in issuing a statement of its position on this subject:

1. Embryos constitute human life.

2. All human beings are made in the image of God and given the breath of life by God alone.

3. Respect for human dignity is paramount in the development of biotechnologies.

4. Cloning human embryos, whether for research or reproductive purposes, must be prohibited.

5. Inheritable genetic modifications [germline changes] must not be allowed.

6. All bioethics research should be motivated by a desire for advancing the health of mankind and not for financial gain.

7. Patent law must not allow for human embryos, genes, cells, and other tissues to become commodities.

8. Genetic information is private to the individual and must never be the basis for discrimination.

9. Fundamental changes in human physiological nature using biotechnology, genetics, nanotechnology, artificial intelligence, and other means must be prohibited.

10. Government funding for research on the ethical, legal, and social issues raised by these new biotechnology developments is essential and must include vigorous oversight and dissemination.[32]

These guidelines were intended to offer what the NAE thought was a reasonable approach to stem cell research, but its claim that "embryos constitute human life" was and is a non-starter, resting as it does on the assumption that life begins at conception. Because, as we have said, this is not an established medical fact, it inserts a religious qualification for scientific research into the most promising of all stem cell lines. For a while evangelicals and the Catholic Church had their way politically when in 2001 President George W. Bush issued an executive order forbidding the use of federal funding in any form of research using embryonic stem cells. But in March of 2009 President Obama overturned the Bush decision, stating:

> In recent years, when it comes to stem cell research, rather than furthering discovery, our government has forced what I believe is a false choice between sound science and moral values.
>
> In this case, I believe the two are not inconsistent. As a person of faith, I believe we are called to care for each other and work to ease human suffering . . . . But in recent years, when it comes to stem cell research, rather than furthering discovery, our government called to care for each other and work to ease human suffering. I believe we have been given the capacity and will to pursue this research—and the humanity and conscience to do so responsibly.[33]

After the President's action, a spokesman for Harvard University's stem cell institute in Cambridge commented, "This will mean the end of the quite onerous bookkeeping and segregation of supplies, equipment and people that were necessary under the Bush executive order. Literally, you could not pick up a pencil off a bench if you were working with embryonic stem cells."[34] Yet with the election of a Republican president the Obama decision might just as quickly be reversed. Protestant and Catholic evangelicals have continued to battle against embryonic and fetal cell research.

32. National Association of Evangelicals, "Resolution."
33. Nasaw, "Obama overturns Bush policy on stem cell research."
34. Ibid.

Since President Obama's decision to allow federal funding of such research the University of Minnesota has been engaged in embryonic stem cell research that includes fetal tissue from elective abortions. In the 2016 legislative session Republicans wanted to withhold 14 million dollars in research funding from the university that would go for the study of addiction, aging, brain imaging, and rural and Native American health unless and until it stopped doing fetal tissue stem cell research. The reason, they said, was to "honor the moral values" of Minnesotans who support the university, but oppose using tissue from aborted fetuses. Their effort failed.

The controversy around stem cell research points to the difficulties posed when evangelical opposition to abortion leads to efforts to control scientific research. This ignores the fact that *science is the search for knowledge*. What to do with that knowledge, how to use it or not use it, invites ethical and moral considerations, but it does not justify placing arbitrary restrictions on the research. What is more, efforts to limit research are destined to fail for the simple reason that someone, somewhere will do it. It would more prudent for the US to be a leader in this field, guided by freedom of thought while also being sensitive to the moral implications of any and all research. This means seeking balance instead of being bound by absolutes, a compromise that moral rigidity simply does not allow.

EVANGELICALISM AND THE RIGHT TO LIFE

Republican evangelicals have also asserted themselves into private lives in regard to right-to-life issues. It is heartwrenching for families having to face the decision about taking a loved one off life support. Is a vegetative state actual life, or does it represent life robbed of all its glorious qualities? Is someone in this state "living" by any reasonable standards? In 2005 Republican evangelicals decided to insert themselves in such a situation that ended up bringing the nation to a near disastrous constitutional crisis.

A Florida woman named Terri Schiavo suffered brain damage in February 1990 when she had a massive heart attack. Eight years after it happened her husband, Michael, sought permission from the 6th Circuit Court of Florida to have his wife's feeding tube removed. The Court ruled in his favor, declaring that the medical evidence confirmed that she was in a persistent vegetative state and the tube could be removed. Schiavo's parents objected and won a temporary court order from a Pinellas County, Florida judge to have the tube reinserted two days later. That was the beginning of a court battle that eventually led to the unprecedented involvement of the US Congress. By signing into law a bill that applied *only* to Terri Schiavo, a dramatic and unprecedented action, Republicans gave federal court jurisdiction over a ruling made by a Florida state court, creating a crisis over the separation of powers and state sovereignty. Before it was over the case had involved the Florida circuit courts, district courts, state courts, federal courts, the Congress, and finally the US Supreme Court.

The politicizing of this family issue and the constitutional crisis it created led to the President and the Congress being severely rebuked by Judge Stanley F. Birch Jr. of the United States Court of Appeals for the 11th Circuit Court, a 1990 George H. W. Bush appointee. Writing in agreement with the court's majority that ruled against the law Congress had passed and President Bush had signed, he said: "When the fervor of political passions moves the executive and legislative branches to act in ways inimical to basic constitutional principles, it is the duty of the judiciary to intervene. If sacrifices to the independence of the judiciary are permitted today, precedent is established for the constitutional transgressions of tomorrow." Further, he said, "legislative dictation of how a federal court should exercise its judicial functions invades the province of the judiciary and violates the separation of powers principle."[35]

One of the most bizarre incidents during this tragedy was when Tennessee Republican Bill Frist, Senate Majority leader and a cardiac surgeon, declared Terri Schiavo was not brain dead based on a video he had seen of her. He was criticized by the medical community for making his diagnosis without even examining the patient in person. Moreover, an autopsy found that Terri's brain was in fact severely atrophied after extensive oxygen deprivation when she had suffered cardiac arrest in 1990, weighing less than half of what it should have, confirming what her attending physicians had maintained all along, that she was in a *permanent* vegetative state.

Surveys at the time showed that Republicans had misjudged what the reaction of the nation would be. More than 70 percent agreed that it was inappropriate for Congress to get involved. Even a majority of evangelicals and Catholics (her parents were Catholic) believed Republicans did what they did in an effort to gain political advantage in the 2006 mid-term elections.[36] And that is precisely the point. At the urging of evangelical lead-

---

35. Goodnough and Yardleymarch, "Federal Judge Condemns Intervention in Schiavo Case."

36. Langer, "Poll: No Role for Government in Schiavo Case."

ers Republicans had taken the country down a dangerous path to score political points. In a democracy there is, of course, nothing that can be done to prevent moral issues from being politicized as they were in this instance, but evangelical partisanship makes it all the more likely to happen in the future, and all the more tragic that religion will likely be used once again to achieve a political goal most Americans do not support.

EVANGELICALISM AND PREMARITAL SEX

In October of 2015 a public meeting in Omaha, Nebraska attended by hundreds of people ended in chaos after shouting and shoving broke out between supporters and opponents of a proposal to update the sex education curriculum that had been in place since 1986. The school board tried again to hold a meeting to discuss the proposed changes in January of 2016. They were told that the new curriculum "rapes children of their innocence." Another person said it was right from "the pits of hell." Supporters said the update was necessary because students needed reliable information that might help lower the rates of teen pregnancy and sexually transmitted diseases that had climbed higher in the Omaha area than the national average. The school board president said that one of the goals of the updated curriculum was to offset the bad information students now get from the Internet about sex-related topics.

It seemed it was the typical fight school boards have faced from parents and even outside groups when sex education has come up. But it is obvious why this particular proposal generated such heated arguments. The topics the updates would add included a discussion of sexual orientation and gender identity in seventh and eighth grades, and discussion of abortion and emergency contraception in tenth-grade lessons on birth control. As expected, on hearing about the proposal a group called Nebraskans for Founders' Values, spearheaded by several evangelical churches in the area, began a campaign to defeat it. The group's mind-set was made clear when its leaders declared that "comprehensive sex education is pornography under the guise of education."[37]

This is the way evangelicals react to sex education in schools because their attitude about premarital sex is more closely aligned to the way people thought about it in the 1950s than the way kids think about it today. Worse, though, is that they have already lost the battle. 30 percent of unmarried

37. Associated Press, "Parents, schools divided as sex ed controversy erupts."

evangelical women between the ages of eighteen and twenty-nine admit to having sex that has resulted in a pregnancy. The Guttmacher Institute says nearly half of all pregnancies in America are unintended and that of the 40 percent that end in abortion, 65 percent involve women who identify themselves as either Protestant or Catholic.[38] In addition, the report found that 42 percent of evangelical singles between eighteen and twenty-nine are currently in a sexual relationship, 22 percent have had sex in the past year, and an additional 10 percent have had sex at least once. This means a bare 20 percent of young evangelical singles in this age bracket have practiced abstinence.[39]

The larger issue of sex before marriage among evangelical teens and youth points to just how ineffective preaching against it is. Abstinence-only programs are failing. This doesn't mean parents and school systems should not discourage premarital sex among teens. Responsible adults know that teens are not mentally and emotionally equipped to cope with what it means to have sex and are certainly ill-equipped to handle pregnancy. Moreover, sex can be dangerous. Sexually transmitted diseases (STDs) are real and teens should be informed of the risks they run when they choose to have sexual relations—especially if unprotected. But once kids reach a certain age the challenge is no longer to keep them abstinent, it is to keep them safe and from having to cope with an unwanted pregnancy.

Obviously, throwing biblical passages at kids doesn't help, not to speak of making the Bible appear irrelevant and out-of-date to teenagers. Candidly, the Bible has little to say that speaks to premarital sex. In that time in history girls were usually married by fifteen. In truth evangelical attitudes most likely arise more from fear than biblical guidance. But fear does not change the fact that the "genie" is out of the bottle and will never be put back in again. Nor perhaps should it. I suggest moral prohibition against premarital sex is not only ineffective, but misguided in the first place, arising as it does from the notion that sex was and is intended to be for procreation only. This is the same argument evangelicals use against homosexuality and is no less misguided. Sex is joyful, pleasurable, delightful, and sometimes results in a baby being conceived. All of it fits together. Reasons for the prohibition of premarital sex don't need more emphasis. The joy of sex does. A healthy and wholesome attitude about it does.

38. Charles, "The Secret Sexual Revolution."
39. Hiestand, "Evangelicals, Premarital Sexual Ethics, and My Grocery List."

Evangelicals who want school districts to teach abstinence are naive. What changes a culture are information and education. Sex education for kids may not be as effective as we would want, but it is a tool that supports a positive relationship parents have with their children that opens the door to honest and informative conversation about sex. Students need more than being told not to have sex. They need to know that the urge to do so is normal, natural, and healthy, but carries enormous responsibilities they should consider before they face them because of carelessness. What happened in Omaha shows the extent to which evangelical attitudes on homosexuality and abortion stand in the way of commonsense attempts to address the realities of sex in the real world in which kids live.

This is one of the reasons evangelicalism has little credibility outside its own circle. Americans are nothing if not pragmatic. They are less interested in ideology than in what works. Evangelical attitudes about premarital sex and sex education in schools have caused conflict in school boards and schools themselves, thus succeeding in making the jobs of principals and teachers that much harder. Again, what drives them are moral beliefs born of fear that usually lead them to have no regard for knowledge from the social sciences or the wisdom among those who work with students every day. Surveys consistently confirm that premarital sex, especially among high school students, is one issue where evangelicals have proven over and again that being right is more important to them than actually making a difference.

* * * * * * * * * * * * * * * *

I would submit that when put in social context evangelicalism's intransigency on moral issues not only causes problems, but is an example of how rigidity creates havoc in the public square. From birth to death and all the years of life in between, absolutes hinder rather than help a society to be moral. Compromise is often the only means by which solutions can be found. It is truly ironic that people who believe in love and peace, forgiveness and reconciliation are the very ones whose views spawn hateful words and actions and force people even in the same families to draw lines in the sand that create separation that can last for years.

It is not surprising that often when evangelicals speak, they are the only ones listening to what they have to say. There is a reason this is the case. That is the focus of the next chapter.

3

CREDIBILITY LOST

THE WORD CREDIBLE MEANS being someone other people have reason to believe or to trust. In the last chapter we examined the intransigency that characterizes evangelical views on issues, and also how their views stand in marked contrast to those of a majority of Americans on every controversial issue we face as a nation. In this chapter we will go the next step and examine in detail why evangelicals are undermining their own credibility, including the tactics they employ to achieve their aims. It will become clear that evangelicals are often their own worst enemy, quick to make bogus claims and engage in behavior that contradicts the demands of justice and peacemaking, all the while ignoring the consequences of political decisions that serve the interests of the few over the good of all. In short, with almost stunning boldness evangelicals have made themselves unreliable stewards of the nation's moral compass.

The sheer number of ways they keep discrediting themselves raises serious question about their capacity for self-reflection. Shooting yourself in the foot multiple times is not the act of a rational person. That evangelicals do this without a second thought could mean that they don't care about what other people think of them, but I believe there is a deeper reason for what they are doing. I suggest it stems from the fact that they have convinced themselves that freedom of religion means beliefs have credibility just because they are religious. It is as if they have completely rejected the notion that reason, logic, and evidence apply to what they say and do as much as they do to everyone else. This may also account for why when their views on moral issues are rejected by the public, the courts, or individuals, they see themselves as victims of intolerance and immediately claim that their religious rights are being violated.

They are wrong. In today's age of mass communications that allows for the most outrageous of religious and political claims being in the news on a daily basis, anyone who speaks must offer reliable evidence to support what they say. Below are the ways evangelicals have ignored that maxim.

ENDS JUSTIFYING MEANS

The statement "ends justify means," is attributed to Niccolò di Bernardo dei Machiavelli's work, *The Prince*, though not without considerable controversy. Machiavelli was a sixteenth-century Italian Renaissance historian and philosopher and considered to be the founder of modern political science. The book's theme is that it is justified for a prince or governing ruler who inherits, seizes, or wins control of a principality to do whatever is necessary for the retention of power. The specific passage in the book from which "ends justify means" thinking sprang says, "let a prince have the credit of conquering and holding his state, the means will always be considered honest, and he will be praised by everybody because the vulgar are always taken by what a thing seems to be and by what comes of it."[1] In his *Discourses* he says, "For although the act condemns the doer, the end may justify him."[2] In both instances Machiavelli is commonly thought to have advocated the axiom that the means by which victory and power are obtained is immaterial because results are the only thing that ultimately matter.

Regardless of what Machiavelli intended to say, the notion that ends justify means is viewed as a philosophy that invites unethical use of power to achieve or retain it. This seems to be a viewpoint widely held among evangelicals in regard to several moral issues, especially abortion. In their view nothing should stand in the way of achieving an end to it, ever how specious the means might be. This is what lies at the heart of the controversy that swirled around the Planned Parenthood videos of 2015. David Daleiden, director of the anti-abortion group, Center for Medical Progress, made videos public that he claimed showed that Planned Parenthood sold abortive fetal tissue for profit.

The conservative political reaction was as predictable as it was immediate. During one of the Republican debates before she dropped out of the presidential race, Carly Fiorina claimed she had viewed the videos and saw "a fully formed fetus on the table, its heart beating, its legs kicking,

1. Machiavelli, *The Prince*, chapter VIII.
2. Machiavelli, *The Discourses* I, 9.

while someone says we have to keep it alive to harvest its brain."[3] This was typical of the reaction from all the Republican candidates. The problem was that the videos were fake. In fact, the deception by the Center for Medical Progress was so egregious that a Houston, Texas grand jury that was initially investigating Planned Parenthood because of the videos not only cleared it of any wrongdoing, but stunned observers by indicting Daleiden and Sandra Merritt, another employee at the Center, on the felony charge of tampering with a governmental record when they used fake California driver's licenses to gain entrance to Planned Parenthood Gulf Coast and to covertly film the video.

Because of the videos several states instituted investigations into Planned Parenthood activities. Texas, Florida, Georgia, Indiana, Kansas, Massachusetts, Michigan, Missouri, Nevada, Ohio, Pennsylvania, South Dakota, and Washington all reported that the charges made in the video were unsubstantiated.[4] Yet Republicans were undeterred by the facts. Reacting to the grand jury decision Fiorina told CNN, "Here's what I know. Planned Parenthood has been trafficking body parts. Planned Parenthood has been altering late-term abortion techniques to this specific purpose of harvesting body parts."[5] Marco Rubio said of the indictment without regard for the grand jury findings, "I'm disturbed . . . I'm disturbed that while Planned Parenthood, who are the ones that were actually selling off these (body) parts were found having done nothing wrong, the people who tried to expose them are the ones that are now facing criminal charges."[6] Ben Carson told CNN that he was "saddened by the decision and equally shocked that they instead decided to indict the individuals that exposed Planned Parenthood's heinous and illegal activities."[7] Former presidential candidate Mike Huckabee reacted to news of the indictments with a Twitter feed that said, "Harvesting human organs is beyond barbaric, it's unimaginably grotesque and evil."[8]

The worst part of Republican refusal to accept the facts about the Planned Parenthood videos is that they have continued to use the deception

3. Quinlan, "Carly Fiorina Stubbornly Stands By Inaccurate Description Of Planned Parenthood Video."

4. Kurtzeleben, "Planned Parenthood Investigations Find No Fetal Tissue Sales."

5. Tesfaye, "Carly Fiorina and GOP frozen in denial over hoax video indictments."

6. Ibid.

7. Ibid.

8. Ibid.

to cut the health organization's funding that hurts poor women who go to Planned Parenthood clinics for health services that include prenatal care, cancer screening, and birth control. Kansas, Arkansas, Louisiana, Alabama, Utah. New Hampshire, Ohio, Wisconsin, Florida, and other states have cut funding or are trying to do so, moves urged by evangelicals. John Stemberger, president of the evangelical Florida Family Policy Council, described the law Governor Rick Scott signed cutting funding to all clinics that provide abortion services regardless of what else they do as "an historic victory against abortion."[9]

Even though federal dollars that support Planned Parenthood *cannot* be used for abortion services, Republicans tried to cut its funding *entirely*, using the fake videos as the reason. Typical of the floor speeches in support of such a bill they passed in September of 2015 was what Rep. Gus Bilirakis, R-FL, said:

> Taxpayers should not be forced to financially support organizations whose behavior is at best unethical and possibly illegal. When it comes to defunding Planned Parenthood, the issue should not be partisan. This is about protecting the rights of taxpayers—but more importantly, protecting the basic right of human life. I will continue to give a voice to our most fragile Americans who cannot speak for themselves.[10]

Attempting to put the issue in proper context, Rep. Diana DeGette, D-CO, responded by saying:

> In fact, there were over 4 million visits to Planned Parenthood clinics last year, and over 90 percent of this was basic women's health care, and not abortions. So why are we talking about this today? Why are we talking about this legislation? Planned Parenthood does these services, and no federal funds are spent on abortion services that Planned Parenthood does provide. But yet the majority will take the radical step of denying women of the basic health care they need. This radical agenda is wrong—it's wrong for American women, and it's wrong for us, when the federal budget expires in just 13 days.[11]

Democrats were able to stop the Republicans from putting these cuts into the overall budget, but until the political life of this false story ends,

9. Cotterell, "Rick Scott Signs Abortion Restrictions Law."
10. Chappell, "House Approves Bill To Cease Funding Planned Parenthood."
11. Ibid.

state and federal efforts to defund Planned Parenthood will continue. In 2016 the Missouri State Senate Committee on the Sanctity of Life subpoenaed consent forms signed by abortion patients it says are necessary for its investigation into Planned Parenthood. The request was rejected. The committee's response was to threaten to jail Mary Kogut, President of Planned Parenthood in the St. Louis area, if she continued to refuse the committee's subpoena of the records. Kogut's lawyers cited federal law protecting patient privacy as the basis for her decision. Win or lose, though, the committee will have succeeded in intimidating Planned Parenthood across the nation, which may have been its intention all along.

The persistent promotion of the Planned Parenthood video story by evangelicals in spite of a growing body of evidence to the contrary points directly to their willingness to follow an "ends justify means" ethic when they believe they are pursuing a higher moral standard. But truth is never sacrificed without consequences to your credibility. The moral chaos an "ends justifying means" philosophy creates is seriously dangerous. Every act of extremism has it defenders, from the shooting of abortion provider Dr. George Tiller by Operation Rescue radical Scott Roeder to Paul Hill's murder of Dr. John Britton and his body guard, James Barrett. These acts and their justification pose an ethical conundrum for evangelical Christians—one that they have yet to be able to maneuver around.

Yet it is one that seems to be inevitable, if not predictable, for them. Journalist and historian of modern conservatism Rick Perlstein says that "ends" are always the primary concern for conservatives, making "means" less important. "If you're a conservative," he observes, "isn't the point of an election to win, so you can bend the world to your will, no matter the means it takes to get there? Even if you don't necessarily have the majority's support?"[12] That's because you will do anything "if you believe you are saving civilization from hurtling toward Armageddon."[13] Not surprisingly one evangelical told Perlstein, "We ought to see clearly that the end does justify the means .... If the method I am using accomplishes the goal I am aiming at, it is for that reason a good method."[14]

The fact that evangelicals have embraced "end justifying means" is rooted in a belief that they can know what God wants and can, therefore, act with a sense of certainty that they are doing the work of God, as Goldwater

12. Perlstein, "Why Conservatives Think the Ends Justify the Means."
13. Ibid.
14. Ibid.

said. But the demands for integrity cannot be dismissed as irrelevant in the pursuit of a higher good. Nations like ours that have engaged in torture of prisoners may have thought that what they considered necessary made it right, as we shall discuss, but they discovered quickly that the rest of the world didn't agree. Evangelicals now find themselves in the same position because of foolishly embracing the ethically discredited philosophy that insists that immoral means can be justified by what is considered moral ends.

DISREGARDING FACTS

Closely related to evangelicals embracing an "ends justifying means" philosophy is that they do not allow facts to have an impact on what they already believe. This can be true of all of us according to Brendon Nyhan, at the University of Michigan, and Jason Reifler, at Georgia State University. Named "backfire," it is a natural defense mechanism to avoid the cognitive dissonance that happens when we are confronted by information that contradicts something we have believed, perhaps for a long time. It is a way, therefore, of coping with having to admit it when we are wrong about something we once believed. It can even lead us to avoid hearing information that we suspect will be different from what we already think.[15]

We see this phenomenon at work, the professors say, when someone refuses to budge from an opinion or belief once it is proven not to be true. I would suggest that evangelicals are the ideal case in point. The fake Planned Parenthood videos is an obvious example, but "backfire" is common among evangelicals on numerous issues. They teach and preach abstinence to teens and young adults in spite of facts that tell them it is not working. They don't want sex education classes to talk about safe sex and using condoms in spite of facts that show teen pregnancy and abortion rates among evangelicals match the rest of the population. They insist homosexuality is a chosen lifestyle in spite of facts that have proven there is a genetic influence on sexual orientation. And on and on.

But it is their antiscience attitude that is the most obvious manifestation of "backfire." Evangelicals seem determined *not* to learn anything from history. When the church has tried to discredit science it has always succeeded in discrediting itself, as was the case when it sanctioned Copernicus and Galileo and later condemned Charles Darwin when his *Origin of the Species* was published. Christian fundamentalists, the forerunners of

15. Conan, "In Politics, Sometimes the Facts Don't Matter." .

today's evangelicals, launched a nationwide campaign to ban the teaching of Darwinism in public schools. In a twist of history it was spearheaded by the three-time Democratic candidate for president, William Jennings Bryan, which eventuated in the now infamous John Scopes Trial in Dayton, Tennessee.

Scopes, a high school biology teacher, was charged with teaching evolution in violation of the Tennessee state law. How the test of the Tennessee anti-evolution law gained traction and how Scopes himself got involved is a story in itself, but the basic issue was whether or not a state could enforce such a law (Bryan had managed to get twenty-five states to pass such laws) without violating the First Amendment that forbids government from establishing a religion. The state won the case, but the fundamentalists lost. The jury found Scopes in violation of the law on the basis of the state having the right to control school curriculum. But it was the trial itself that made the biggest impression on the public, especially the moment when Scopes's defense attorney Clarence Darrow called Bryan himself to the stand as an expert witness regarding the Bible even though he was the prosecuting attorney for the state.

Darrow's intention was to use the great Bryan as a means to undermine a literalist interpretation of the Bible. Under a barrage of questions about characters and events in the Bible, Darrow managed to get Bryan to admit that some things in the Bible should not be taken literally. That was the opening Darrow needed. From that point on he trapped Bryan into answering questions he didn't want to answer, but could not avoid without seeming evasive. The two men engaged in heated exchanges to the point where the judge finally adjourned the trial until the next day. When court reconvened, he reversed his own ruling and would not allow Bryan to be called again as a witness for the defense. In addition he ordered Bryan's testimony from the previous day to be stricken from the trial record. Eventually Bryan won a verdict against Scopes, but the damage to biblical literalism had been done. In the public's eyes it was a moralistic form of Christianity that was simply too antiscience to be taken seriously.

Fast forward almost forty years to Little Rock, Arkansas and a young woman named Susan Epperson who was hired to teach tenth-grade biology at Central High School. She was herself a product of the Arkansas school system and later attended college and then graduate school at the University of Illinois, where she received her master's degree in zoology. Prior to her joining the Central High faculty, the biology textbook being used excluded any mention of evolution because Arkansas was one of the two remaining states that had a law making the teaching of evolution illegal (Mississippi was the other). Adopted in 1928 just after the Scopes trial, the Arkansas law forbade the teaching of any theory that suggested human beings had evolved from any other species. This law applied to state universities as well as public schools.

At the beginning of the 1965–66 school year Susan was confronted with a career-changing dilemma. On recommendation of the teachers of biology the Little Rock school administration approved the use of a text-book that included a chapter on evolution. Susan knew that based on state law she could be dismissed for using it in her biology classes. What was she to do? Not use the text the school system had adopted, use it but not teach the chapter on evolution, or teach it as it was? At the urging of the state teachers association she chose another course. Under the guidance of legal counsel, she filed a lawsuit in the Chancery Court of the State to have the Arkansas statute declared void. She also requested that the state be forbidden from having her contract terminated. A parent of one of the children, H. H. Blanchard, intervened in support of Susan's action.

The State Chancery Court ruled in Susan Epperson's favor. It stated that the Arkansas statute was a direct violation of the Constitutional guarantee of freedom of speech and thought contained in the First Amendment. The statute, the Chancery Court said, "tends to hinder the quest for knowledge, restrict the freedom to learn, and restrain the freedom to teach."[16] Thus, the court invalidated the statute based on the First Amendment that prohibits states from requiring, in the words of the majority opinion, "that teaching and learning must be tailored to the principles or prohibitions of any religious sect or dogma."

On appeal the Arkansas State Supreme Court reversed the Chancery Court ruling, but on the basis that the state had the rightful power to specify school curriculum in its public schools. The Court did not address the question as to the constitutionality of the statute itself that had been the basis for the Chancery Court ruling.[17] The ruling meant that Susan Epperson could not use the textbook she was told to use or could not teach the chapter on evolution since the interpretation of the statute as argued by the state was that "if Mrs. Epperson would tell her students that 'Here

16. *Epperson v. Arkansas.*
17. Ibid.

is Darwin's theory, that man ascended or descended from a lower form of being' . . . she would be, under this statute, liable for prosecution."[18]

Her attorney appealed the state court's decision to the United States Supreme Court, which heard arguments in October, 1968, and rendered its decision in November. The Justices clearly saw this case as one going to the heart and soul of the Constitution, most especially the First Amendment that involved the distinction between individual and religious freedom. In a unanimous opinion overturning the Arkansas Court ruling, Justice Abe Fortas concluded his writing of the Court's ruling as follows:

> Arkansas' law cannot be defended as an act of religious neutrality. Arkansas did not seek to excise from the curricula of its schools and universities all discussion of the origin of man. The law's effort was confined to an attempt to blot out a particular theory because of its supposed conflict with the Biblical account, literally read. Plainly, the law is contrary to the mandate of the First, and in violation of the Fourteenth, Amendments to the Constitution.[19]

One interesting note about this case is the fact that the Little Rock Ministerial Association, with mostly mainline clergy members, supported Susan Epperson in her lawsuit. After the decision a Presbyterian minister who had written a book about the Scopes trial arranged for Susan, her husband, and her father to meet with John Scopes and his wife, Mildred. In the conversation she recalled learning that during her trial Scopes himself had received letters telling him what he had been told at the time of his own trial, that he was going to hell. In fact, he received more letters during Epperson's court case than she received.[20]

After the Arkansas law was struck down, evangelicals realized their fight against modern science had to go in another direction. Instead of opposing the teaching of evolution altogether, they decided to promote teaching what they called "creation science" alongside the teaching of evolution. The Institute for Creation Research, located in Dallas, became the primary advocate for this dual curriculum approach, and with some success. Several states chose it as a middle ground to appease evangelical voters without abandoning science altogether. That came to an abrupt, and perhaps permanent, halt in Dover, Pennsylvania in 2005.

18. Ibid.

19. *Epperson v. Arkansas.*

20. American Civil Liberties Union, "Reconciling Faith and Evolution in the Classroom."

The curriculum creation science uses tries to make the case that the traditional principle of "randomness" cannot fully explain the extensive and verifiable "order" that exists in the universe. Creationists insist that what does explain such "order" is "intelligent design," a cousin theory to creation science that says there are certain features of the universe and of living things "best explained by an intelligent cause, not an undirected process such as natural selection." Creationists further contend that through the study and analysis of a system's components they can determine "whether various natural structures are the product of chance, natural law, intelligent design, or some combination thereof."[21] If what they say is true it might qualify as "science," but if not then "creation science" would be another name for religious beliefs.

The test case that would determine the answer legally took place in Dover, Pennsylvania when the local school district board voted six to three to allow lectures to be given to ninth grade students about the theory of intelligent design and to make available a book entitled *Of Pandas and People: The Central Question of Biological Origins*, which promoted intelligent design and included direct challenges to evolution. The board justified its actions with a statement that read in part:

> Because Darwin's Theory is a theory, it is still being tested as new evidence is discovered. The Theory is not a fact. Gaps in the Theory exist for which there is no evidence. A theory is defined as a well-tested explanation that unifies a broad range of observations.
>
> Intelligent design is an explanation of the origin of life that differs from Darwin's view. The reference book, *Of Pandas and People,* is available for students to see if they would like to explore this view in an effort to gain an understanding of what intelligent design actually involves.[22]

The board also instructed the schools to add a statement to their biology curriculum that said: "Students will be made aware of the gaps/problems in Darwin's theory and of other theories of evolution including, but not limited to, intelligent design. Note: Origins of life is not taught."[23]

In response eleven parents of Dover students sued the school district over its decision. The suit, *Tammy Kitzmiller, et al. v. Dover Area School District, et al.*," was filed in the US District Court for the Middle District of

---

21. Center for Science and Culture, "Intelligent Design."
22. Jones, Middle District of Pennsylvania, Tammy Kitzmiller, et al. .
23. Ibid.

Pennsylvania. The plaintiffs sought declaratory and injunctive relief regarding the school policy. It was the first case of its kind that challenged the teaching of intelligent design in a public school. It was a bench trial (no jury) with the Honorable John E. Jones as the presiding judge. The arguments came down to this question: was the school board within its power to enact the policy as part of its responsibility to "enhance science education," as it claimed, or was it guilty of allowing religious instruction to be given at a public school under the guise of "science"? Judge Jones heard arguments from the end of September through the first of November, 2005, and then rendered his decision in December of that year. His ruling was a strong rebuke of evangelical insistence that "creationism" is science:

> Although as noted Defendants have consistently asserted that the ID (Intelligent Design) Policy was enacted for the secular purposes of improving science education and encouraging students to exercise critical thinking skills, the Board took none of the steps that school officials would take if these stated goals had truly been their objective. The Board consulted no scientific materials. The Board contacted no scientists or scientific organizations. The Board failed to consider the views of the District's science teachers. The Board relied solely on legal advice from two organizations with demonstrably religious, cultural, and legal missions, the Discovery Institute and the TMLC (Thomas More Law Center). Moreover, Defendants' asserted secular purpose of improving science education is belied by the fact that most if not all of the Board members who voted in favor of the biology curriculum change conceded that they still do not know, nor have they ever known, precisely what ID is. To assert a secular purpose against this backdrop is ludicrous.
>
> Accordingly, we find that the secular purposes claimed by the Board amount to a pretext for the Board's real purpose, which was to promote religion in the public school classroom, in violation of the Establishment Clause.
>
> The citizens of the Dover area were poorly served by the members of the Board who voted for the ID Policy. It is ironic that several of these individuals, who so staunchly and proudly touted their religious convictions in public, would time and again lie to cover their tracks and disguise the real purpose behind the ID Policy.
>
> This case came to us as the result of the activism of an ill-informed faction on a school board, aided by a national public interest law firm eager to find a constitutional test case on ID, who

in combination drove the Board to adopt an imprudent and ultimately unconstitutional policy.

The breathtaking inanity of the Board's decision is evident
when considered against the factual backdrop which has now
been fully revealed through this trial. The students, parents, and
teachers of the Dover Area School District deserved better than to
be dragged into this legal maelstrom, with its resulting utter waste
of monetary and personal resources.[24]

This ruling underscores the problems evangelicals cause when they
refuse to recognize, understand, or accept the distinction between faith
and facts. The Dover school system was thrust into a controversy not of its
own making solely because evangelicals had no respect for that distinction.
Without question the students, parents, and teachers of the Dover Area
School District did deserve better than to be dragged into the legal maelstrom evangelicals created.

Mark Noll says evangelicalism deserved better as well. In chapter 5
we will discuss in detail the damage Noll says fundamentalism has done
to evangelicalism, but we can say here that his own assessment of creation
science would likely support the ruling Judge Jones rendered. "Creation
science," he says, "has damaged evangelicalism by making it much more
difficult to think clearly about human origins, the age of the earth, and
mechanisms of geological and biological change." He continues, "But it
has done more profound damage by undermining the ability to look at the
world God has made and to understand what we see when we do look."[25]

Evangelicals today do not think, though. Their minds are closed. They
know what they know without knowing what they don't know.

RELIGIOUSLY FREE TO DISCRIMINATE

In 1964 Lloyd Maurice Bessinger Sr. was a businessman who owned four
barbecue restaurants in West Columbia, South Carolina. He was also a
staunch segregationist. When Mrs. Anne Newman, the wife of an African
American minister, tried to enter one of his restaurants she was turned
away. She sued on the basis of the Civil Rights Act of 1964. By 1968 the case
had reached the US Supreme Court, which rendered a decision in favor of
Mrs. Newman. The Court also awarded her legal fees based on Title II of

24. Ibid.
25. Noll, *The Scandal of the Evangelical Mind*, 196.

the Civil Rights Act. In the words of the ruling, "Congress therefore enacted the provision for counsel fees—not simply to penalize litigants who deliberately advance arguments they know to be untenable but, more broadly, to encourage individuals injured by racial discrimination to seek judicial relief under Title II."[26]

Bessinger never accepted the Court's decision as just, stating publicly, "It is really a constitutional right whether a man has the right to run his business without governmental interference."[27] He also believed his freedom of religion was violated by the Court ruling, his attorney stating in the appeal of the lower court decisions against Bessinger that the 1964 Civil Rights Act "was invalid because it 'contravenes the will of God' and constitutes an interference with the 'free exercise of the Defendant's religion.'"[28] "I'm just a fair man," Bessinger said. "I want to be known as a hard-working, Christian man that loves God and wants to further (God's) work throughout the world as I have been doing throughout the last 25 years."[29]

If this justification for the right of a business owner to refuse service on the basis of religious beliefs sounds familiar, it should. It is the same argument being made today to justify "religious freedom" laws being passed in a growing number of states to allow business owners to refuse service to same-sex couples. Promoted by evangelical groups such as the Alliance Defending Freedom, the American Family Association, the Becket Fund for Religious Liberty, and the Family Research Council, in 2015 the Indiana state legislature became the first to enact such a law. Its Religious Freedom Restoration Act established a legal basis for individuals and businesses to refuse service to anyone on the basis of their personal religious beliefs. As Sections 8 & 9 of the law state:

> (a) . . . a governmental entity may not substantially burden a person's exercise of religion, even if the burden results from a rule of general applicability. (b) A governmental entity may substantially burden a person's exercise of religion only if the governmental entity demonstrates that application of the burden to the person: (1) is in furtherance of a compelling governmental interest; and (2) is the least restrictive means of furthering that compelling governmental interest.

26. *Newman v. Piggie Park Enterprises.*

27. Monk, "Barbecue eatery owner, segregationist Maurice Bessinger dies at 83."

28. *Newman v. Piggie Park Enterprises.*

29. Ibid.

> A person whose exercise of religion has been substantially burdened, or is likely to be substantially burdened, by a violation of this chapter may assert the violation or impending violation as a claim or defense in a judicial or administrative proceeding, regardless of whether the state or any other governmental entity is a party to the proceeding.[30]

The Indiana law sprang from the federal Religious Freedom Restoration Act born of a conflict over the right to use peyote in Native American spiritual practices. Two Oregon men, Alfred Smith and Galen Black, were counselors at a private drug rehabilitation clinic when they ingested peyote during one of the religious ceremonies of the Native American church to which they belonged. At the time possession of peyote was a crime under Oregon law. When the treatment center learned of this practice, the two were fired. When they filed a claim for unemployment compensation with the state, they were turned down on the basis that their dismissal was deemed work-related misconduct. Smith and Black took their case to court, ultimately reaching the US Supreme Court, where they lost. In an opinion written by Justice Antonin Scalia, the Court affirmed the right to the exercise of religious freedom, but ruled that it could not be used in this instance as a reason not to obey the Oregon ban on peyote because the state law applied to everyone and not solely to them. Scalia went further and accused the men of using their right to the free exercise of their religion as an excuse to ingest peyote.

The Supreme Court ruling prompted Congress to act to correct what members believed was an assault on religious freedom. With the support of then President Bill Clinton, the Senate and House passed the federal Religious Freedom Restoration Act. Its purpose, the act stated, was "(1) to restore the compelling interest test as set forth in Federal court cases before Employment Division of Oregon v. Smith and to guarantee its application in all cases where free exercise of religion is substantially burdened; and (2) to provide a claim or defense to persons whose religious exercise is substantially burdened by government."[31] But in 1997 the Supreme Court ruled that while the law applied at the federal level, it was not within the powers of Congress to enforce its provisions in the states.

That decision opened the door for and at the same time invited states to pass their own versions of a religious freedom restoration act. Indiana

30. Indiana Religious Freedom Law.
31. Religious Freedom Restoration Act.

did and nineteen others have followed suit or are seeking to do so. But there is a significant difference between these state laws and the one passed by the Congress. The federal law applies only to individual rights being "substantially burdened by the government," whereas state laws do the reverse. They apply to a business claiming it is being "substantially burden" by an individual who wants to prevent it from exercising its religious freedom.

The larger social context for the law was the issue of evangelical businesses having to serve same-sex couples because of a 2006 lawsuit in New Mexico. That case involved Vanessa Willock suing Elaine and Jonathan Huguenin, a New Mexico couple who owned Elaine Photography, for refusing to photograph a commitment ceremony between her and her same-sex partner, Misti Collinsworth. Willock's complaint was based on the fact that the New Mexico Constitution's Human Rights Act had been revised in 1972 to offer equal protection to people regardless of sexual orientation, but evangelicals viewed the decision as setting a precedent for business owners being forced to go against their anti-homosexual beliefs.

The Huguenins argued that they did not want to convey through pictures a conflicting "understanding of marriage." In their view photography was a form of artistic expression. Because of their anti-homosexual beliefs as Christians, they believed they should be free to refuse to give such artistic expression to a same-sex couple's commitment ceremony. Willock's attorney, Tobias B. Wolff, a University of Pennsylvania law professor, argued that businesses were public enterprises that had to abide by anti-discrimination laws. "Whatever service you provide," he said, "you must not discriminate against customers when you engage in public commerce." Once a company begins selling its goods to the public, he argued, "it is not a private actor engaged in the expression of its own message. Customers do not pay for the privilege of facilitating the company's message. Customers pay to have their own event memorialized."[32]

The New Mexico Supreme Court agreed, citing the state's Human Rights Act of '72 that prohibits discrimination on the basis of sexual orientation as a basis for its decision. My reading of the opinion led me to conclude that the court tried to render a balanced and fair ruling, confirmed by the concurring opinion written by a member of the court, Justice Richard Bosson. Bosson's opinion was a beautifully written legal statement, if such a thing is possible, that expressed genuine sympathy for the position Elaine

32. Barnes, "Case weighing religious freedom against rights of others is headed to Supreme Court."

and Jonathan Huguenin were in because of what they believed, but also explained unequivocally why the Court could not rule in their favor.

> Jonathan and Elaine Huguenin see themselves in much the same position as the students in Barnette (a 1943 case in which the Supreme Court held that the State of West Virginia could not constitutionally require students to salute the American flag and recite the Pledge of Allegiance). As devout, practicing Christians, they believe, as a matter of faith, that certain commands of the Bible are not left open to secular interpretation; they are meant to be obeyed. Among those commands, according to the Huguenins, is an injunction against same-sex marriage. On the record before us, no one has questioned the Huguenins' devoutness or their sincerity; their religious convictions deserve our respect.[33]

Citing the Supreme Court ruling in the *Loving v. Virginia* interracial marriage case, Justice Bosson noted that there is a lesson to be drawn from what the Supreme Court said:

> There is a lesson here. In a constitutional form of government, personal, religious, and moral beliefs, when acted upon to the detriment of someone else's rights, have constitutional limits. One is free to believe, think, and speak as one's conscience, or God, dictates. But when actions, even religiously inspired, conflict with other constitutionally protected rights—in Loving the right to be free from invidious racial discrimination—then there must be some accommodation.[34]

He was cognizant and respectful of the fact that the Huguenins were not trying to prohibit Willock and Collinsworth from marrying, that they simply wanted to be left alone to conduct their photography business in a manner consistent with their moral convictions. But, he goes on to say, their desire had a larger context that could not be ignored.

> On a larger scale, this case provokes reflection on what this nation is all about, its promise of fairness, liberty, equality of opportunity, and justice. At its heart, this case teaches that at some point in our lives all of us must compromise, if only a little, to accommodate the contrasting values of others. A multicultural, pluralistic society, one of our nation's strengths, demands no less. The Huguenins

33. Gillman, Graber, and Whittington, "American Constitutionalism, Supplementary Material."

34. Ibid.

are free to think, to say, to believe, as they wish; they may pray to the God of their choice and follow those commandments in their personal lives wherever they lead. The Constitution protects the Huguenins in that respect and much more. But there is a price, one that we all have to pay somewhere in our civic life.[35]

It is at this point that Justice Bosson brings his opinion to a close with words that might well be characterized as inspired.

In the smaller, more focused world of the marketplace, of commerce, of public accommodation, the Huguenins have to channel their conduct, not their beliefs, so as to leave space for other Americans who believe something different. That compromise is part of the glue that holds us together as a nation, the tolerance that lubricates the varied moving parts of us as a people. That sense of respect we owe others, whether or not we believe as they do, illuminates this country, setting it apart from the discord that afflicts much of the rest of the world. In short, I would say to the Huguenins, with the utmost respect: it is the price of citizenship. I therefore concur.[36]

This opinion by Justice Richard Bosson reflected genuine wisdom that could serve as a guide to the nation in balancing religious freedom in the marketplace and the demands of equal protection under the Constitution. As attorney Sherry F. Colb wrote of Justice Bosson's concurring opinion:

It is rare for courts to offer this sort of statement of appreciation for the inconvenient fact that abiding by laws—even laws that most of us consider just, right, and expressive of what is best about American culture—exacts a non-trivial cost from those who nurture strong commitments that conflict with those laws. For those of us in the majority (as well as the minority), this empathy is worth nurturing toward those whose priorities and values differ drastically from our own.[37]

It seems that these remarkable insights of Justice Bosson point the way forward on issues of this nature. Compromise is, as he so eloquently said, "part of the glue that holds us together as a nation." The kind of nation we are is tested when priorities and values do differ and even clash. Are we a

35. Ibid.

36. Ibid.

37. Colb, "The New Mexico Supreme Court Applies Anti-Discrimination Law to Wedding Photographer."

nation that permits one group of people to experience discrimination on the basis of another's religious beliefs, or are we people who understand that personal beliefs are never threatened when actions contribute to everyone being treated the same under the law? Evangelicals take the former view, when the latter seems far more reasonable and accommodating of our nation's diversity.

As expected, extremists have started engaging in their mischief since these laws have been passed. Jeff Amyx, owner of Amyx Hardware & Roofing Supplies in Grainger County, Tennessee, immediately after the Supreme Court ruling on gay marriage put a sign outside his store that read, "No Gays Allowed." Later he changed the sign to read, "We reserve the right to refuse service to anyone who would violate our rights of freedom of speech & freedom of religion."[38] But he has no regrets about the sign. Claiming to also be a Baptist minister, he says, "I don't hate people. It's not the people I hate, it's the sin that I hate."[39]

Such examples are dismissed by evangelicals as exceptions, not the rule, just as they refuse to see the connection between the argument Lloyd Maurice Bessinger Sr. made on religious grounds for refusing to serve African Americans in his barbecue restaurants in South Carolina and evangelicals claiming the right to refuse service to homosexuals. Yet setting the arguments for religious freedom laws being made today alongside the arguments used in the '60s to justify racial discrimination gives the distinct impression that refusing to acknowledge the similarity is intentional. The only difference between them is that one involves race and the other relates to sexual orientation. One of the hallmark achievements we have made as a nation is to choose to include everyone in the constitutional guarantee that liberty and justice are for all. The 1964 Civil Rights Act is an unequivocal expression of that decision.

In this context, the best that can be said about evangelicals promoting religious freedom laws is that they represent tone deafness. As a nation we still have a long way to go to overcome racial discrimination, but we have come far enough to know that when discrimination raises its ugly head in any way, we will not tolerate it even when it is justified on the basis of the exercise of religious freedom.

38. "Tennessee hardware store puts up 'No Gays Allowed' sign."

39. Chan, "Tennessee hardware store owner posts 'No Gays Allowed' sign on front door."

BOGUS PERSECUTION

The evangelical war on the mythical "war on Christmas" is an annual spectacle fueled by commentators on Fox News. The latter is in fact where it all began when Bill O'Reilly started talking about people saying "Happy Holidays" instead of "Merry Christmas." It was a sign, he said, of a conspiracy by secular progressives fighting against the Judeo-Christian tradition "because that stands in the way of gay marriage, legalized drugs, euthanasia, all of the greatest hits on the secular progressive play card." Their goal, he said, is to get "religion out of the public arena."[40]

Evangelicals immediately picked up on O'Reilly's theme. The "war on Christmas," they said, was the reason schools no longer allowed Christmas pageants, Christmas carols, and Christmas trees. Secularists, the insist, have even gotten schools to replace "Christmas Holidays" on their calendar with "Winter Break." It's all part of a grand scheme to rid the nation of Christian influence, co-opting businesses into supporting it. Evangelicals want people who "shop 'til they drop" to be greeted with "Merry Christmas" as they leave the store instead of some bland "Happy Holidays." O'Reilly opined that store owners should be more grateful for Christmas than they are. "Every company in America should be on their knees thanking Jesus for being born. Without Christmas, most American businesses would be far less profitable. More than enough reason for business to be screaming 'Merry Christmas.'"[41]

In 2015 Starbucks became the focus of a viral war because of its decision to discontinue using holiday images on its coffee cups. "Starbucks hates Jesus" was the charge evangelical preacher Joshua Feuerstein made in a video he posted on his Facebook page. Listening to his rant was like watching a child throw a temper tantrum, but it got more than eleven million views. His goal was to start a nationwide boycott of Starbucks until it caved to his demands. It didn't happen, not least because mythical wars seldom gain traction beyond a radical few who make a lot of noise, but who eventually show themselves to be as foolish as they actually are.

At its core the mythical "war on Christmas" is symptomatic of evangelicals continuing to reject the fact that Christianity is not the official religion of the United States. There was a time as a nation when we acted as if it were. Everything about life in my hometown of Lynchburg, Virginia

40. Gill, *Media Matters*.

41. Gibson, *The War On Christmas*, xxiii–xxiv.

was organized around Christianity in ways that showed no awareness of or respect for the Jewish community (Muslims were invisible back then). There was only one synagogue in my hometown. I knew it was there, knew the name of the rabbi, and knew his son personally as a classmate of mine. But I did not know that when the all-white high school football team played its home game every Friday night it was on the Jewish Sabbath. I paid no attention to the fact that every prayer uttered in the schools I attended were Christian or that the prayer at the football games was delivered by Christian clergy only. Student assemblies were opened with student led devotions, all Christian. The speaker for the annual football banquet was usually someone who played in the NFL and spoke at an all-student assembly the morning of the banquet. One year Raymond Berry, the former pro receiver for the world champion Baltimore Colts, spoke to the students and ended his remarks by saying that he was not really there to talk about football, but to talk about Jesus Christ as his lord and savior.

This was America at a time when we had not learned what it meant to actually live by the Constitution our founders had written, a time when Christianity was the de facto national religion, and anyone of another faith was tolerated only because they were not seen or heard. Then things changed. A woman of no faith, atheist Madeline O'Hara, began to challenge the nation's public religiosity in courts that had no choice but to make rulings based on the Constitution instead of social norms, and when lower courts didn't, the Supreme Court did. And that changed the world I grew up in and helped us to become more mature as citizens than we had been.

As the nation moved away from its excessive accommodation of Christian holy days and practices, evangelicals began labeling bans against Christian manger scenes on public property and schools no longer sponsoring pageants about the birth of Jesus as a "war on Christmas." But most Americans see it for the sham it is. They would not be upset to hear a store clerk wish them a merry Christmas, but they also understand the reason "happy holidays" has become a substitute. After all, churches still enjoy the right to set up manger scenes on their lawns, hold Christian pageants, sing Christmas carols, offer prayers of thanksgiving, and hold Christmas Eve worship services all day long. Most people are not going to spend much time fuming over something as unimportant as what a person says to you during the holidays as you pass them on the street.

In a country that has a Christian majority, with more than 65 percent of Americans still identifying themselves as "Christian," where streets of every city, town, hamlet, and country lane are lined with churches, and when hundreds of thousands come out to hear the Pope speak wherever he goes, it is a hard sell for evangelicals to convince the public that Christianity is under attack by secular humanists. Making matters worse for them are their words and actions aimed at denying some Americans the civil rights all other Americans enjoy because of their sexual orientation or their gender. With that kind of track record it is no surprise that after more than ten years of fighting the "war on Christmas," no one is paying attention.

GUNS IN CHURCHES

A survey taken in 2012 found that only 38 percent of white evangelicals support stronger gun control laws, compared to 60 percent of the religiously unaffiliated. It also reported that almost 60 percent of those same white evangelicals already have a gun in their home.[42] These are the people who instigated and now support the "Mississippi Church Protecting Act," or what the media is calling the "guns in churches" law, that allows armed guards to carry weapons in churches to protect worshippers. The justification for this particular law was said to be the killing of nine black worshippers during a Bible study session at a church in Charleston, South Carolina in 2015. "Churches deserve protection from those who would harm worshippers," Republican Governor Phil Bryant said after he signed the bill.[43]

Since laws like this are often written by outside groups and offered around the country, it is likely that more states will probably follow Mississippi's example. For all practical purposes evangelical churches have bought the NRA mantra that the only thing that can stop a bad guy with a gun is a good guy with a gun. The inconsistency of such a position with the life and teachings of Jesus is obvious even to a casual reader of the Bible. Indeed, there is a startling paradox in the picture of the people Jesus told to turn the other cheek carrying guns into sanctuaries built to honor God for the sole purpose of protecting themselves against a possible attacker. This is not the kind of image that easily disappears from people's minds. Instead it lingers as they wonder how to reconcile guns in churches that are lined with crosses. The gospel doesn't compel Christians to be foolish, but neither

42. Pew Research Center, "Slim Majority of Americans Support Passing Stricter Gun Control Laws."

43. Gates, "Miss. law allows churches to train members to pack heat."

does it justify bowing to the gods of culture that lure them into trusting the wisdom of the NRA over the power of non-violence.

I wrote on this subject in one of my blogs and received the following response from one reader

> "It's up to us older guys and gals to support the church to help the younger generation know Christ.
>
> Our church of about 1000, average age is probably about 30. Our "Gatekeeper" group is about 50 years old (average). Most of us are armed. All of us go through annual training and testing. We are a covert group, but most everyone knows we're around. 6 are active PD of some sort, 1 is retired PD, 5 are security guards of some sort and 3 are past Marines. We are all CPR qualified. We practice active shooter, fire and tornado drills annually. We've had some divorce, child custody, temporarily lost child, gas leak, drug and stalking issues. If you don't have issues in your church of that size, your (sic) just kidding yourself and being an ostrich.
>
> We get a discount on our insurance since we are pro active in our concerns for the "Safety" of our flock. We may be wrong, but we'll just have to let God sort that out . . .
>
> Our pastor was threatened because he tried to counsel a couple over their separation/divorce. The guy blamed him for their divorce and came for him drunk and armed with a firearm. Our pastor thought about quitting since it scared him so badly and to be honest "rocked" his beliefs to his core. Thank God he decided his teaching expertise is still in use helping lost people to come to Christ the American way."

At the time I had no words with which to respond to this man, believing as I do that you cannot take out of someone's mind with reason what reason didn't put into it in the first place. His faith was too Americanized for him to realize how contradictory his words are to the words of Jesus. Sadly, though, he reflects the way many evangelicals think about guns. I will have more to say about this in the final chapter, but it needs to be underscored here that despite its claim of being biblically based, evangelicalism teaches and preaches an Americanized gospel that has not only lost its way, but its soul, yet another reason it has lost credibility when it speaks about moral issues.

CONDONING TORTURE

The late William Sloane Coffin, Yale University Chaplain during the turbulent 1960s and a major leader in the American peace movement, was lecturing on the US possession of nuclear weapons when he made the observation, "We may have the power to destroy humanity, but we have not been given the moral authority to do so."[44] In a single sentence Coffin named the most difficult thing for citizens of any nation to remember when their government begins to make a case for war—that war is always a moral issue. Fear has a way of pushing moral concerns out of people's minds, making possible what American writer Barbara Ehrenreich calls war's "epidemicity," or "the tendency of war to spread in the manner of an infectious disease."

> Obviously, war is not a symptom of disease or the work of microbes, but it does spread geographically in a disease-like manner, usually as groups take up warfare in response to war-like neighbors. It also spreads through time, as the losses suffered in one war call forth new wars of retaliation . . . the idea of a war to end war is one of its oldest, and cruelest, tricks nations can pull on their people.[45]

There may be no more graphic example of "epidemicity" than the US war on terror that keeps spreading like a fire fueled by information that stokes the fears of all Americans that any day a terrorist will blow up a plane, an airport, a train station, a school, a government building, or something else. As our fears are fed our capacity to think rationally and morally about what our government is doing diminishes. History is filled with stories of once peaceful nations, communities, and individuals acting in ways no less barbaric and cruel than the enemies they have to fight. In the truest sense war becomes a sign of the insanity and inhumanity of which all people are capable when fear controls their minds and closes their hearts.

The most egregious act of such insanity and inhumanity by our own government in the most recent past (at least we hope it is "past") is the torturing of suspected terrorists during the George W. Bush administration promoted and perhaps even directed by Vice President Dick Cheney. In 2014 the United States Senate Intelligence Committee released part of a massive report on the CIA torture of prisoners of war. That report provided

44. Coffin, lecture.
45. Ehrenreich, "Disease of Our Making."

detailed documentation of the absolute brutality and lawlessness of what the CIA did in the name of security. It all began when the Bush administration turned to military psychologists James Mitchell and Bruce Jessen to develop an interrogation program based on the exploitation and abuse of CIA captives. What they developed violated the Geneva Convention of 1949 that established humanitarian laws regarding the treatment of prisoners of war in the hope that they would help prevent what happened during WWII from happening again. The US established similar laws to ensure we would set an example for the rest of the world.

The "enhanced interrogation" program Mitchel and Jessen developed and the CIA carried out violated international law and the moral code of conduct we had set for ourselves as a civilized nation. The goal was a complete psychological breakdown of prisoners through prolonged isolation, sleep deprivation, sensory deprivation and overload, forced nudity and sexual humiliation, and, of course, water-boarding or simulated drowning. In short, the United States of America that had prided itself as a moral example for the world betrayed everything we once stood for all because we were so afraid that we could not collectively think clearly about what we were willing to do as a people.

The justification for what we did was that the CIA was able to obtain critical information that prevented additional attacks on our country and saved many lives. Only those involved in the torture program make these claims. Experienced interrogators have totally rejected such claims, arguing that torture is a waste of valuable time because people being tortured will say anything to make it stop, while the torturer has no way of knowing whether what is said is true or false. In point of fact, the Senate report itself disputed the reliability of CIA claims about the information gained, including the fact that CIA operatives lied outright about information they said they received. What is more, innocent people were tortured by methods too horrible for description.[46]

In response to the Senate Report President Obama released a statement that said in part:

> The report documents a troubling program involving enhanced interrogation techniques on terrorism suspects in secret facilities outside the United States, and it reinforces my long-held view that these harsh methods were not only inconsistent with our values as a nation, they did not serve our broader counter-terrorism efforts

46. Volsky. "17 Disgraceful Facts Buried In The Senate's 600 Page Torture Report."

or our national security interests. Moreover, these techniques did significant damage to America's standing in the world and made it harder to pursue our interests with allies and partners. That is why I will continue to use my authority as president to make sure we never resort to those methods again.[47]

Inexplicably, evangelicals supported what the CIA did, and still do. A 2009 survey found that 62 percent said torture is often or sometimes justified. Another 17 percent said it could be used "rarely." Only 16 percent said torture was never justified. Most revealing is that the survey found that the percentage of evangelical support for torture was higher than the general population and the percentage of evangelicals rejecting torture was smaller.[48] In 2014 when the Senate report on torture was released a *Washington Post* survey asked evangelicals if they believed CIA "enhanced interrogation" of suspected terrorists was justified. 69 percent rejected calling "enhanced interrogation" "torture." In addition it found that the split between how evangelicals and the general population viewed torture mirrored the divide between Republicans and Democrats, suggesting what we have said before, that evangelical political affiliation has more influence on their moral positions than their religious beliefs do.[49]

These survey results show that evangelical views about torture represents the most extreme elements of the Republican Party rather than the more balanced, and I would say, more moral, views of Republican Senator John McCain. A former Vietnam prisoner of war, McCain took to the Senate floor on December 9, 2014, to deliver a moving speech in support of the release of the Senate Intelligence Committee Report on torture, during which he explained the reasons our nation should not have ever engaged in it.

> Mr. President, I rise in support of the release—the long-delayed release—of the Senate Intelligence Committee's summarized, unclassified review of the so-called "enhanced interrogation techniques" that were employed by the previous administration to extract information from captured terrorists. It is a thorough and thoughtful study of practices that I believe not only failed their purpose—to secure actionable intelligence to prevent further

47. Parsons, "Obama says report shows CIA torture program at odds with U.S. values."

48. Pew Research Center, "The Religious Dimensions of the Torture Debate."

49. Posner, "Christians More Supportive of Torture than Non-Religious Americans."

attacks on the U.S. and our allies—but actually damaged our security interests, as well as our reputation as a force for good in the world.

He continued:

> I know from personal experience that the abuse of prisoners will produce more bad than good intelligence. I know that victims of torture will offer intentionally misleading information if they think their captors will believe it. I know they will say whatever they think their torturers want them to say if they believe it will stop their suffering. Most of all, I know the use of torture compromises that which most distinguishes us from our enemies, our belief that all people, even captured enemies, possess basic human rights, which are protected by international conventions the U.S. not only joined, but for the most part authored.

Toward the end of this stunning speech Senator McCain said:

> . . . in the end, torture's failure to serve its intended purpose isn't the main reason to oppose its use. I have often said, and will always maintain, that this question isn't about our enemies; it's about us. It's about who we were, who we are and who we aspire to be. It's about how we represent ourselves to the world.[50]

Therein is the lesson evangelicals should have never ignored. Just as the United States has paid a severe price for engaging in torture, so have evangelicals for their support of it, perhaps irrevocably so.

MORAL MYOPIA

The general meaning of the word *myopic* "is a lack of foresight or discernment or a narrow view of something." Among all the reasons evangelicals lack credibility when they speak, the fact that they manifest the condition of "moral myopia" is probably the major one. Symptomatic of their myopia is a failure to understand the moral significance of Republican voter disenfranchisement and Republican refusal to admit that climate change/global warming demands urgent attention.

Concerning the former, in 2006 Congress renewed the 1965 Voting Rights Act that had made the "one man, one vote" principle a reality for

---

50. McCain, "Floor Statement by Senator John McCain on Senate Intelligence Committee Report."

every American citizen regardless of race. Section 5 of that law required certain states to receive "preclearance" approval by the Justice Department for any changes in voting procedures before they can take effect. Section 4b set out the preclearance formula that determined which states (nine in the South) would have to meet Section 5 requirements. The purpose of both sections was to ensure that states in the deep South that had been so egregiously discriminatory could not enact laws to circumvent the Voting Rights Act. Originally that provision was to expire after five years, but each time Congress has reauthorized the act it has determined that sufficient evidence supported Section 4 and 5 also being renewed, as was again the case in 2006.

In February of 2013 Shelby County, Alabama petitioned an exemption from the "preclearance" provision and was turned down. The county lost each of its appeals in lower courts and finally won approval from the Supreme Court to hear its case. The Supreme Court's conservative majority ruled in favor of Shelby County and struck down Sections 4 and 5 of the original Voting Rights act. Chief Justice John Roberts wrote the majority opinion and stated the reason for it as follows:

> Nearly 50 years later, things have changed dramatically. Largely because of the Voting Rights Act, "voter turnout and registration rates" in covered jurisdictions now approach parity. Blatantly discriminatory evasions of federal decrees are rare. And minority candidates hold office at unprecedented levels . . . . The tests and devices that blocked ballot access have been forbidden nationwide for over 40 years. Yet the Act has not eased 5's restrictions or narrowed the scope of 4's coverage formula along the way. Instead those extraordinary and unprecedented features have been reauthorized as if nothing has changed, and they have grown even stronger.[51]

In light of the fact that "times have changed," Roberts said, the Court reversed the decision of the lower courts to uphold the decision by Congress in 2006 to renew sections 5 and 4 when it renewed the Voting Rights Act itself and ruled in favor of Shelby County.

The decision was widely criticized as failing to understand the fact that residual prejudice and discrimination remained a significant factor in regard to voting rights. That criticism proved prescient when within twenty-four hours of the decision five of the nine states that had been under

51. *Shelby County v. Holder.*

"pre-clearance" requirements took steps to alter their voting laws (Virginia, South Carolina, Mississippi, Alabama, and Texas). Encouraged by a 2002 "Help America Vote Act" passed by Republicans and signed by President Bush that required a photo or non-photo ID for all first-time voters in presidential elections, Republican legislators in the above states sought to enact laws that required a photo ID for *all* voters to register and to vote in *all* elections. Critics of the content of the laws argued that they would place unjustified burdens on minorities, the elderly, and the young. Reflecting on the Supreme Court upholding an Indiana voter ID law passed in 2008, Justice John Paul Stevens who wrote the "lead opinion" later called it "a fairly unfortunate decision."[52]

The Brennan Center for Justice at New York University School says that since 2010 Kansas, Wisconsin, Nebraska, New Hampshire, Rhode Island, Ohio, Florida, Georgia, North Carolina, Tennessee, and Arizona have joined Indiana and the five states mentioned earlier in passing such laws. Thus far the ID requirements have been extremely uneven in terms of what constitutes an acceptable photo ID and whether or not special IDs are free. Texas, for example, made the decision to accept IDs for weapons permits, but rejected college IDs. Some ID laws have been struck down, others upheld. More important, though, is that according to the Government Accountability Office (GAO) five of ten academic studies report that ID laws have led to a drop in voter participation by as much as 4 percent in some areas. The worst instances of a drop in voting were in Kansas and Tennessee.[53]

But the core issue is why the push for voter IDs after the 2013 Court ruling? For supporters the argument for them is a simple one. IDs will prevent voter fraud. Yet not one state has produced reliable evidence that supports the claim that fraud is real. Moreover, in 2007 after a five-year investigation by the Bush administration to determine to what extent voter fraud was a problem, the investigation "turned up virtually no evidence of any organized effort to skew federal elections."[54] According to Rutgers political scientist Lorraine Minnite, who wrote a book on the subject, "the best facts we can gather to assess the magnitude of the alleged problem of voter fraud shows that, although millions of people cast ballots every year,

52. Barnes, "Stevens says Supreme Court decision on voter ID was correct, but maybe not right."

53. Wihbey, "Voter ID laws and the evidence."

54. Nyhan, "Voter Fraud Is Rare, but Myth Is Widespread."

almost no one knowingly or willfully casts an illegal vote in the United States today."[55] In addition, the Government Accounting Office reported that the Justice Department had stated in a recent court filing that after reviewing its databases and other records that there were "no apparent cases of in-person voter impersonation charged by DOJ's Criminal Division or by U.S. Attorney's offices anywhere in the United States, from 2004 through July 3, 2014."[56]

Perhaps the only voter fraud that actually exists are voter fraud laws themselves, especially when the laws that have been passed do not even address the particular claims of voter fraud that have been made. In 2004, for example, Ohio Republican Secretary of State Ken Blackwell instituted strict rules that made churches and other not-for-profit groups afraid of conducting voting registration drives because of the threat of facing felony charges if they made a mistake. He also created havoc over provisional ballots by issuing arbitrary rules that placed the responsibility on poll workers to determine who was eligible even though no such determination was required beyond a person signing a statement to that effect. What is more, he issued a rule that said voter registration cards not printed on eighty-pound stock would be rejected without any explanation as to why this was needed. His actions were criticized by public officials and news analysts as an effort to suppress the vote in Ohio. In not one instance did his actions address the specific ways voter fraud might have happened had it actually been a problem.

The same can be said about the 2015 decision by the governor of Alabama to restrict the hours several DMV offices were to be open, most of which were located in the counties with the highest percentage of non-white registered voters—Macon, Greene, Sumter, Lowndes, Bullock, Perry, Wilcox, Dallas, Hale, and Montgomery (Dallas and Montgomery were slated for complete shutdown under the governor's plan). It was no secret that this decision had nothing to do with state budget cuts as the governor claimed. It was all about limiting voting. The voter ID law the state passed required a DMV picture ID only to register and to vote.

Laws like this impose serious burdens on older voters who cannot easily travel to a court house or DMV office to obtain a photo ID, who live on very limited budgets, and many of whom may not have birth certificates required to receive an ID. Also, when people move the address on their

55. Minnite, "The Misleading Myth of Voter Fraud," 6.
56. Wihbey, "Voter ID laws and the evidence."

driver's license is no longer accurate, and that is an automatic disqualification from voting in many states. This creates a special problem for students who vote where they attend college, but have a driver's license from their home state. In addition, cutting back on voter registration days and places, along with voting hours (as Florida did in dramatic fashion in 2012), has proven to lead to unthinkably long lines for the people who actually show up to vote. For the poor who often hold two and three jobs and have limited time in between, this is especially difficult.

Viewed in its entire context, it becomes obvious that voter suppression is about morality as much as it is about politics. Discrimination in any form is morally destructive to individuals and to a nation. The only prominent evangelical leader I am aware of who has addressed this issue is Jim Wallis, but his voice, though important, is muted as an evangelical because his stands on other issues such as abortion and gay marriage have essentially labeled him as a progressive whether he wishes to be one or not. If we are to accept on face value the sincerity of evangelicals in speaking about moral concerns they believe our country must confront, where is the justification for not using their considerable influence among Republican leaders to try to stop state legislators from subverting the right to vote among minorities and others? I have no doubt that had state legislators heard evangelical leaders speaking against voter suppression proposals some, perhaps many, would have never been enacted into law.

But evangelicals could have done even more. They could have chosen to follow the example of the Rev. Dr. William Barber and his Moral Mondays movement. This was an effort over a two-year period wherein Christians and non-Christians gathered at the North Carolina capitol to protest the backwards, discriminatory, and callous policies of the North Carolina legislature, laws such as voting rights restrictions, state budgets that cut education and state run social safety net programs, and an unjustified refusal to expand Medicaid under Obamacare that would provide insurance to the poorest of the poor. Thousands of Christians have chosen to join Rev. Barber in speaking on behalf of those who have no voice, but noticeably absent are any prominent evangelical leaders in the state.

They could also support one of their own, Republican Representative Jim Sensenbrenner of Wisconsin, in his effort to revise the pre-clearance formula as the Supreme Court instructed. Thus far he has yet to get the House Republican leadership to bring the bill to the floor for a vote. Recently he wrote an op-ed piece for the *New York Times* that explained why Congress needs to pass the bill.

If Congress doesn't act soon, 2016 will be the first time since 1964 that the United States will elect a president without the full protections of the law. Modernizing the act to address the Supreme Court's concerns should be one of Congress's highest priorities.

Enacted in 1965, the Voting Rights Act began a healing process that ameliorated decades of discrimination. It is vital to this country's commitment to never again permit racial prejudice to determine who has access to a ballot.

One of the law's core protections is its preclearance system. Before the law's passage, states and local governments would discriminate against minority voters, Congress or courts would ban the discriminatory practices, and states would find new ways to discriminate.[57]

He goes on to explain succinctly and cogently why those who say "preclearance" is no longer necessary are simply wrong, especially when they argue that the courts and/or the public always have the chance to redress any voter discrimination that is discovered. "There is no adequate remedy," he wrote, "for voter discrimination after an election because there is no way to know who would have won absent discrimination. Preclearance prevents discrimination before it affects elections."[58]

Sensenbrenner was a member of the House Judiciary Committee that recommended the reauthorization of the Voting Rights Act in 2006. He noted in his *Times* piece that during hearings the Committee "amassed a legislative record of more than 15,000 pages in which it documented discrimination" against voters that left no doubt about the need for the Act to be reauthorized in full. "Ensuring that every eligible voter can cast a ballot without fear, deterrence and prejudice is a basic American right," he wrote, concluding, "I would rather lose my job than suppress votes to keep it."[59]

Sensenbrenner is a man of integrity, and his position on voting rights is a morally principled stand, but he is an exception in today's Republican Party. His bill has 100 cosponsors, but of that number only thirteen Republicans have signed on.[60] What if evangelicals used their political muscle to persuade House Republicans to support their colleague in this effort? They won't, it seems, perhaps because they are afraid to do anything that in the long run would weaken their influence for garnering votes on the kind

57. Sensenbrenner, "Suppress Votes? I'd Rather Lose My Job."

58. Ibid.

59. Ibid.

60. Pew Research Center, "How the Faithful Voted."

of divisive moral issues they focus on. Instead of doing something for the common good, they choose to do something that has no potential for doing the country any good.

****

Denying the reality of climate change and the effects of global warming is not more important than the issue of voter disenfranchisement, but it is clearly more urgent because of the increasing threat it poses to the entire world's social, economic, and political stability. The signs that something dire is happening are legion. Sixteen inches of rain fell in a twelve-hour period in the Houston, Texas area on April 18, 2016. Before it was over more than twenty-four inches had fallen causing devastating flooding that left thousands homeless. At least five deaths related to the flooding were reported, but that number would likely increase, officials said. The only thing even remotely like what happened was caused by tropical storm Allison in 2001. This storm was nothing unusual except for its size. It left over fifty-six inches of snow in the Colorado mountains near Denver before hitting Houston in the form of rain. By the time it reached Texas the storm was 21,000 square miles wide.

This kind of storm with a magnitude virtually unheard of would have been called historic only a few years ago. Today it is becoming commonplace. The warmest fifteen years recorded for the globe have been since the turn of the century. Only one year during that period didn't set a record. In 2016 all the scientists studying the melting rate of the polar ice caps in the Antarctic and Greenland agreed in one joint statement that over the last twenty years the melt had been rapid, with the Greenland ice cap declining faster than the Antarctic. Melting affects the rest of the world directly by rising sea levels as fresh water is pushed into the sea and dramatically changing ocean currents.

Another sign of what is happening is that 93 percent of the Great Coral Reef off the coast of Australia is bleached. This means most of it is white, caused by warming ocean temperatures, indicating the corals are expelling the algae (zooxanthellae) living in their tissues, putting them at serious risk of dying. The Great Coral Reef consists of 2,900 individual reefs and 900 islands stretching over an area that is approximately 133,000 square miles. It is teeming with literally billions of tiny organisms called "coral polyps." It is easily identifiable from outer space. And the evidence is mounting that global warming is killing it. Professor Terry Hughes, head of the ARC Centre of Excellence for Coral Reef Studies at James Cook University, issued a statement in which he said, "I showed the results of aerial surveys of bleaching on the Great Barrier Reef to my students, and then we wept."[61]

According to an article posted on the *Scientific American* website some of the facts about climate change and global warming are these:

- carbon dioxide, a by-product of fossil-fuel combustion, is a greenhouse gas, which traps solar radiation in the atmosphere

- Increased human fossil-fuel consumption over the past two centuries has increased levels of carbon dioxide in the atmosphere. Atmospheric CO_2 recently surpassed 400 parts per million, the highest level in more than 800,000 years.

- As a result of increases in atmospheric carbon dioxide, global surface temperatures have increased by about one degree centigrade since 1880.

- Reasonable extrapolations from current trends suggest that unchecked fossil-fuel consumption will increase the risk of coastal flooding, droughts, severe storms, heat waves, food and water shortages and other harmful effects.

- A consensus of scientific experts believes that fossil-fuel consumption is driving global warming.

- The United States, historically, has been the biggest emitter of carbon dioxide and hence bears the greatest responsibility for climate change.

- Those who agree that climate change poses a threat vehemently disagree about how severe the threat is, how it should be countered and how it should be discussed in public.[62]

Given the evidence and scientific consensus that exists, denial of climate change and global warming is a sign of willful ignorance, along with denying the human factors that are contributing to both. The only thing in question is the extent of the damage that has already been done and whether any of it can be reversed. That is why common sense suggests that the wisest course of action is to assume the worst and hope/work for the best.

61. Mooney, "'And then we wept.'"
62. Horgan, "Climate Change: Facts Versus Opinions."

The point of addressing this subject here is not to debate climate change per se, but to point out that for people of faith climate change/global warming demand attention because they are moral issues. The impact of the severe storms we are seeing already means that thousands of lives are being affected, and in too many instances lost. Moreover, the poor of the world are always affected the most because they live in areas that are most vulnerable to storms and floods. The poor in New Orleans suffered the worst when Katrina hit, and still are to this day. Yet this moral issue does not seem to show up on the evangelical radar screen except among those who read *Sojourners* magazine or belong to Evangelicals for Social Action. *Sojourners* says that 60 percent of evangelicals believe climate change is real and that human beings are making things worse. At the same time it admits what other surveys have found, that political affiliation has more influence on evangelical views on climate change than their religious beliefs.[63]

In a survey taken in 2015 the Pew Research Center found that only 6 percent of the American population said their religious beliefs were a major factor in their views on climate change. Almost everything else, from political affiliation to the news media to friends to family, had more influence on them. But contrary to what *Sojourners* reported, Pew found that only 28 percent of evangelicals believe the earth is getting warmer because of human activity. Seventy percent attributed any warming of the earth to natural causes or said that there was no solid evidence that it was happening at all.[64]

The least we can say about what evangelicals think about climate change and global warming is that they seem relatively unconcerned about it, and that is the point I want to underscore. Given their passion about abortion, same-sex marriage, and gender use of restrooms, evangelicals show little interest in justice for the creation. They are not alone in ignoring climate change that may turn out to be the greatest challenge humanity faces in this century, but their insistence that our nation is in moral decline rings hollow when this kind of issue goes unnoticed by them. Playing the role of the moral police for the nation places you in the position where to choose one moral issue, but ignore others undercuts anything and everything you say.

Making things worse is the fact that evangelical beliefs are contributing to climate change/global warming denial. Evangelical Republican Senator

63. Schmitt, "Talking to Evangelicals About Climate Change."
64. Funk and Alper, "Religion and Views on Climate and Energy Issues."

James Inhofe of Oklahoma, well known for calling global warming a hoax (he published a book in 2012 titled *The Greatest Hoax: How the Global Warming Conspiracy Threatens Your Future*) was asked in a radio interview about his biblical views on global warming. He replied, "God's still up there. The arrogance of people to think that we, human beings, would be able to change what He is doing in the climate is to me outrageous."[65] The fact that Inhofe's largest campaign contributions come from the oil and gas industry may be as much as factor in his view of global warming as what he believes the Bible says, but in public he connects his religious beliefs to public policy. Curiously the Republican Senate majority named Inhofe Chairman of the Environment and Public Works Committee, a not-so-subtle indication of what they also think about climate change/global warming.

No person can speak quickly, forthrightly, unequivocally, and certainly not rightly on every issue a nation faces, but evangelicals can do better than silence in the face of what responsible political leaders, scientists, theologians, and millions of ordinary citizens believe is the greatest moral issue facing the world today. Jesus talked about "the weightier matters of the law" (Matt 23:23). It's difficult to imagine that destroying the planet does not fall into that category. Admittedly there are some evangelicals who understand the moral dimensions of climate change, but they left the evangelical fold in everything but name a long time ago. What seems odd is the fact that evangelicals don't realize that there are consequences to their own behavior. Being religious places a special responsibility on people to be responsible when they speak or act. A common weakness among all religions is the assumption that to speak of the things of God exempts the one speaking of the need to speak reasonably and humbly.

Actually, evangelicals seem to embody two extremes—speaking too much and speaking too little. Calling the moment a bill was signed into law that gave businesses a legal basis for discrimination against homosexuals or transgender individuals "a great day" does not witness to moral convictions. It witnesses to intolerance and judgmentalism. Remaining silent as the negative effects of climate change or voter laws become more and more apparent is a living reminder of moral myopia. Both erode confidence in what evangelicals believe and raise questions about the political motivation behind their moral stands.

65. Rozsa, "Inhofe says the Environmental Protection Agency is 'brainwashing our kids.'"

As bad as the erosion of credibility is, the damage it has done is not limited to undercutting evangelical moral pronouncements. It also reflects a level of bad politics and bad religion that should concern all of us. That is the subject to which we now turn our attention.

4

WHY PARTISAN EVANGELICALISM
IS BAD POLITICS

IN THE FIRST THREE chapters we have talked about evangelicalism and evangelicals when closer to reality is the fact that, as Jason Bivins points out, we are talking about "evangelicalisms."[1] Evangelicalism is a tradition of great complexity."[2] I realize, therefore, as I have talked about evangelicals thus far what I have been doing is offering a "suggestive interpretation of some evangelicals, some beliefs, some practices, a reading that stimulates thought about the whole without presuming to stand for it."[3]

In deference to this fact, as we move to the subjects of "bad" politics and "bad" religion in this chapter and the next, the term "partisan evangelicalism" will appear throughout in both. Yet the fact remains that even in acknowledging its diversity, evangelicals themselves do hold in common specific beliefs to an extent that warrants using "evangelicalism" when discussing the extremes it has produced in both American politics and American Christianity. This justification for using the word is augmented by sufficient polling data that has accurately measured how evangelicals think and what they believe. "Partisan evangelicals" are those who are consciously or de facto members of the Republican constituency most often referred to as "the evangelical vote." They are both politicians themselves and/or their supporters who elect and keep them in office.

1. Bivins, *The Religion of Fear*, 214.
2. Ibid.
3. Ibid.

BAD POLITICS

On January 24, 2013, Texas Republican Senator Ted Cruz ended his twenty-one-hour filibuster of a funding bill to keep the government from shutting down. He was protesting the fact that Obamacare was included in the budget. Defund it or shut the government down, he declared. That was the choice. His colleagues did not agree. In fact, Senate procedural rules prevented Cruz's filibuster from achieving its goal, something Cruz knew would happen before he started. That is why his short-circuited filibuster was widely seen as a campaign tactic for his anticipated 2016 run for the Republican presidential nomination that in the end he lost to Donald Trump.

At one point during his filibuster, Cruz compared everyone who opposed his position as being "like Neville Chamberlain, who told the British people, 'Accept the Nazis.'" Arizona Republican Senator John McCain found that offensive and said as much after the filibuster: "I resoundingly reject that allegation. To allege that there are people today who are like those who, prior to World War II, didn't stand up and oppose the atrocities that were taking place in Europe, because I have an open and honest disagreement with the process ... is an inappropriate place for debate on the floor of the United States Senate."[4]

Appropriate or not, what Ted Cruz, a self-avowed evangelical Christian whose father is an evangelical minister, said on the floor of the US Senate reflected then and now the state of American politics. Decorum, respect for others, refraining from engaging in personal attacks, these once well-established political norms are gone. Divide and conquer seems to be the rule. In his book *Where Do We Go From Here*, Martin Luther King Jr. tells the story of a famous novelist whose papers were discovered in his home after his death. Among them was a list of suggested plots for novels he might one day write. One of them was, "A widely separated family inherits a house in which they have to live together."[5] Dr. King was talking about the "world house" in which all of us now live. I want to focus on the house we live in called the United States.

At the moment we are a very separated, divided family, and evangelicals have played no small role in getting us to this place. Our national government is in stalemate where little business of the people gets done. Working "across the aisle" is rare, and when it does happen it often leads to

---

4. Milbank, "Ted Cruz's phony Obamacare filibuster was really about ... Ted Cruz."
5. King, *Where Do We Go from Here*, 167.

Republican incumbents facing primary challenges from candidates appealing to the worst instincts of Republican voters. States under GOP control have made radical right turns in promoting an aggressive moral agenda intended to circumvent laws related to abortion, same-sex marriage, gender identity, and placing arbitrary restrictions on the precious right to vote. In many ways we are "the *United* States" in name only.

The divided nation we have become was never more apparent than when John Boehner, Republican Speaker of the House, extended an invitation to Israeli Prime Minister Benjamin Netanyahu to speak before a joint session of Congress in 2015 without any consultation with the White House. The purpose of the invitation was to give Netanyahu, the leader of a foreign nation, an opportunity to make a case against President Obama's planned nuclear arms treaty with Iran. It was the first time in the history of our nation that such an egregious violation of protocol had happened. "Unprecedented . . . hitting below the belt" is how Professor Guy Ziv of American University described it. Having studied US-Israeli relations for years, he said the invitation represented "taking partisanship to a whole new level. It is a way for them to embarrass and humiliate the Obama administration."[6]

Netanyahu was facing a tough reelection campaign in his own country and many observers thought he accepted such an unprecedented invitation to boost his standing in the eyes of Israeli voters. Writer Jeffrey Goldberg of *The Atlantic*, known for his hawkish position on Iran, questioned why Netanyahu would ever think it was appropriate to so publicly challenge the Obama administration. His answer was that it looked like an attempt by Netanyahu to boost his reelection chances.[7] Even prominent Israelis criticized the speech as irresponsible and fraught with danger. Chuck Freilich, a former deputy head of Israel's National Security Council, said Netanyahu was risking undermining relations with the United States in a misguided attempt "to mobilize Congress against the administration, . . . a highly irresponsible act doomed to failure."[8]

Being the uncritical supporters of Israel they are, evangelical political and religious leaders defended the Netanyahu invitation in spite of what it said about the divided state of our own nation. In the end the speech had no effect on the President's negotiations with Iran and the deal was signed

6. Scott, "Boehner's Netanyahu Invite Is An 'Unprecedented' Diss Of Obama."

7. Ibid.

8. Tharoor, "The case against Netanyahu's speech to Congress."

later in the year, but it did mark a new low in American political history. Any other time the decision would not have stood, but a divided nation could not bring sufficient pressure to bear on Speaker Boehner to act more responsibly. It would seem we have reached the point where no bridge is too far for partisanship to cross.

FUTILE MORALS REGULATION

One of the reasons partisan evangelicals play such a dominant role in dividing the nation is that they have convinced themselves they are battling for the soul of America and that the political power of the Republican Party is the key to winning that battle. The enemy is "secularism," a strange thing since the word simply means "not religious," or "relating to the worldly or temporal." Yet in the eyes of evangelicals "worldly" means "ungodly," even "evil." What it comes down to is that anything and everyone who disagrees with what evangelicals believe and believe in is considered "ungodly," even "anti-god." This has a long history. In his informative book, *The Evangelical Origins of the Living Constitution*, John Compton documents their efforts at what he calls "morals regulation" reaching back to the early 1800s just after the ratification of the US Constitution.

Before the Revolutionary War the colonies had allowed various forms of "morals regulation," especially in New England where Puritanism tried in every way possible to control moral behavior. The picture of people locked in stocks and on public display captured that period in our history. From public drunkenness to gambling to adultery to Sabbath breaking, Puritanism was determined to maintain what it defined as communal moral standards, earning H. L. Mencken's description of Puritanism itself as "the fear that someone, somewhere, may be happy."[9]

Almost a century later the US Constitution seemed to ensure that a Puritan worldview would not control the nation's public square. But, as Compton says, evangelicals had other ideas. The Second Great Awakening inspired an early nineteenth century religious revival that inspired evangelicals to try to rid the new nation of all manner of vice, especially the consumption of alcohol and the use of lotteries. The problem was that the Constitution focuses on protecting individual and corporate rights while saying nothing about regulating public morality. That task was left to the states with one critical caveat. State law could not undermine or abrogate

9. Elliott, foreword.

constitutional guarantees of rights as spelled out in its text. Three of them that clashed with "morals regulation" were the right to "property, contract, and commerce."[10]

No one could have anticipated the collision course that a nationwide religious revival would put evangelicals on with the Constitution. Businesses benefited from alcohol sales and institutions such as colleges benefited from lotteries. Both groups challenged evangelical anti-vice laws in court and won. Needless to say the glory of the new Constitution lost its luster among evangelicals unhappy with court rulings. Compton says they came to believe that the founders had "struck a deal with the Devil" when they wrote the Constitution and in the process had "mortgaged the nation's soul in a bid for national prosperity."[11]

Lotteries were the first flash point in the conflict. Initiating a lottery involved a state legislature entering into an agreement with an institution such as a college that would last as long as it took to raise the designated amount of money set as the goal. Such agreements usually included provisions for the recipient of the grant to provide bonds and sureties, pay out winning tickets in a timely fashion, and keep its books open for state inspection. Grants such as these literally numbered into the hundreds with many of them still in process when the Second Great Awakening gave birth to the "morals regulation" movement.

Compton recounts the story of the New York state legislature passing a statute "imposing high license fees on lottery ticket vendors and requiring all vendors to post bonds and find sureties to guarantee good behavior."[12] Evangelicals had lobbied for the new regulations and hailed its passage as a triumph over a national vice. New York Governor DeWitt Clinton believed the bill was unconstitutional even though he expressed sympathy for it. A few years earlier the Supreme Court under Chief Justice John Marshall had already ruled in favor of Dartmouth College when the state of New Hampshire tried to redraw the college's corporate charter. That decision confirmed the inviolability of contracts made under the Constitution's Contract Clause. Clinton believed that lottery grants had the same constitutional protections that all contracts did and so he chose to veto the bill rather than spending money to defend it.[13] Because of the veto the

10. Compton, *The Evangelical Origins of the Living Constitution*, 21.

11. Ibid, 4.

12. Ibid., 41.

13. Ibid.

case did not settle the constitutional question about lottery regulations, but Compton says it did highlight "the emerging disjunction between popular morality and entrenched constitutional ideals."[14]

Massachusetts got into the fray when pro-temperance evangelicals persuaded the legislature to pass the "Fifteen Gallon Law" that forbid the sale of alcohol in anything less than fifteen gallons. The intention was to put the numerous small taverns out of business by requiring them to purchase overly large amounts of alcohol. A major effort to repeal the law began as soon as it was signed into law. Two years later a new governor was elected who persuaded the legislature to do just that.[15] But the fight over alcohol was far from over in the eyes of evangelicals. They scored a major victory when the Congress passed the Eighteenth Amendment to the Constitution that prohibited the manufacturing, storage in barrels or bottles, transportation, sale, possession, and consumption of alcohol and the states ratified it in record time. The Congress had set aside seven years for ratification. It took only eleven months. In 1918 the nation had embraced the National Prohibition Act, and in October of 1919 a commission to see to its implementation met to draw up the regulations for enforcement.

For those who favored the law it worked effectively, mainly in small towns and rural America. For those who didn't, mainly in urban areas, it was ignored. Speakeasies, clubs that sold alcohol illegally, bootlegging, and private moonshining became ways around Prohibition. Arising from a genuine concern over increasing public drunkenness and alcoholism, Prohibition advocates overplayed their hand in convincing voters that the amendment was the way to deal with the problem. The by-product was a crime-infested underground that made millions of dollars selling alcohol illegally. One estimate is that Chicago crime boss Al Capone made $60 million from bootlegging and speakeasies.[16]

By 1932 Prohibition had grown very unpopular, not least because people of means still had access to alcohol whereas poor people could not afford bootlegging prices. Republican President Herbert Hoover, who had called Prohibition "the great social and economic experiment, noble in motive and far reaching in purpose," was handily defeated by Franklin Roosevelt, who had run on a platform that included repealing the Eighteenth Amendment. Early in 1933 he got Congress to pass the proposed

14. Ibid.
15. Ibid., 43–46.
16. "Prohibition."

Twenty-first Amendment to the Constitution that would do just that, and the states ratified it in less time than they had approved Prohibition fourteen years earlier.

One of the ironies of the court decisions about lotteries and alcohol that so disturbed evangelicals was the fact that they were based on an "original intent" philosophy of constitutional interpretation. The Constitution's focus on individual rights and the absence of anything in it that involved the regulation of moral vices was the basis for jurisprudence in the early 1800s not being at all friendly to evangelical beliefs. This, Compton says, led them to become advocates of what we think of today as a "living Constitution" philosophy, the interpretative approach that viewed the Constitution "as a 'living' document whose key provisions should be understood to evolve in tandem with moral and economic development of the nation."[17]

Compton's provocative account of the tension and conflict between evangelical "morals regulation" and the Constitution's concern for the protection of rights puts today's partisan evangelicalism in a very helpful historical context. The founders authored a Constitution that gave us a federal system of jurisprudence that has remained a flash point between conflicting federal and state decisions regulating personal morality through moral laws. Prohibition at the national level had shown the dangers inherent in "morals regulation" on a large scale, but that did not stop evangelicals from trying at the local level. As the nation's churches doubled their membership and the number of clergy increased dramatically, there was enormous pressure on state and local politicians to regulate and, if possible, eliminate the sale of alcohol and lottery tickets.[18]

Similar efforts continue today. The similarity between "morals regulation" in the nineteenth and early twentieth century and today's evangelical sponsored TRAP laws being passed today by Republican legislatures is striking. It's not that morals don't matter in the public square or that evangelical moral teachings should be abandoned. Instead, the issue is always about methods. There are many Americans, for example, perhaps a large majority, who desire to see fewer and fewer women choosing to have an abortion. But they reject making that choice altogether illegal because in their eyes abortion is a moral decision individuals have a right to make for themselves within certain boundaries.

17. Compton, *The Evangelical Origins of the Living Constitution,* 11.
18. Ibid., 20.

History suggests that evangelicals have believed since the beginning of our constitutional form of government that morality regulated by the state takes precedence over personal choice. Since the late 1970s they have worked through the Republican Party to achieve that end on every controversial moral issue we have faced.

A POLITICAL GOD

On the face of it, the notion that anyone would think that Republicans are God's pick of political parties is ridiculous, but it may not be as absurd as it seems. Recall the fact that in naming their preferred presidential candidates not one of the one hundred most prominent evangelical leaders in the nation chose a Democrat. The survey didn't cite the reasons why this was the case, but it is possible that many of them believed Democrats were anti-God, or at minimum too secular to be Godly.

This opinion actually exists among evangelical Republicans. The 2013 Republican candidate for Lt. Governor in Virginia repeatedly said this was his view. Reverend E. W. Jackson, a minister and a lawyer who also sought the Republican nomination for the US Senate in 2012, said that believing in God and voting Democratic were incompatible. When asked to explain what he meant, he responded: "I said it because I believe that the Democrat Party has become an anti-God party, I think it's an anti-life party, I think it's an anti-family party. And these are all things I think Christians hold to very dearly."[19]

In February 2015 blogger Rod Dreher reacted to Democrats blocking a bill in the Colorado legislature that would have allowed religious clubs on state college campuses to set rules on faith for their leaders. He wrote *The American Conservative* website: "Many of us simply do not trust Democrats and liberals when it comes to safeguarding our religious liberty . . . . I believe that there is nothing the Democratic Party won't do to religious believers in the name of advancing LGBT rights."[20] A post on the *Sean Hannity Show* website Forum Board on April 2, 2015 began with the words: "The Democratic Party Has Officially Become The Anti-Christian Party." It then listed the reasons why this was true. Among them was: "They keep

---

19. Seitz-Wald, "The 'anti-God' party."
20. Dreher, "Democrats as the Anti-Christian Party."

going after Christians, Churches, Christian holidays, & Christian owned businesses . . . [and] the Democrats won't stop there."[21]

A more nuanced view of Democrats being anti-God came from a popular evangelical blogger named Jack Wellman. He said that he didn't rule out voting for a Democrat, but would only if they followed a simple guide he used for all candidates:

> I choose to vote for candidates for their position on the sanctity of life. If they support a ban on abortion (save for the life of the mother), then I usually vote for them. God is pro-life because He is the Author of it. He alone has the right to decide when a person is born and when they should die. I vote my conscious [sic]. I do not vote on the candidate with the best platform like lower taxes. To God, there is a sanctity to life and I believe we should vote to protect those who cannot protect themselves.[22]

Given the fact that since *Roe v. Wade* (1973) no Democratic candidate for President nor any prominent Democrat in the Senate or House leadership has stood against that decision, the writer was de facto saying that only Republicans stand with God in regard to being "pro-life." Offered as a more "reasonable" position on whether Democrats are Christian or not, Wellman's view also ends up making Democrats "anti-God."

These comments are from people who hold modest standing in the public arena and probably have a limited circle of evangelicals on whom they exert influence. But their views reflect the way a large number of evangelicals think about the differences between Republicans and Democrats, augmented by the Republican Party Platform they believe reflects a "pro-God" position on moral issues. Yet reading the Platform itself suggests that its "beauty" for evangelicals may lie more in the eye of the beholder than in fact. The various section heads are:

1. A Restoration of Constitutional Order: Congress and the Executive

2. Defending Marriage Against An Activist Judiciary

3. A Sacred Contract: Defense of Marriage

4. Living Within Our Means: A Constitutional Budget

5. Federalism and The Tenth Amendment

6. The Continuing Importance of Protecting the Electoral College

21. Hannity, *The Sean Hannity Show,* April 2, 2015.

22. Wellman, "Are Christians Republicans or Democrats?"

7. Voter Integrity to Ensure Honest Elections

8. The First Amendment: The Foresight of Our Founders to Protect Religious Freedom

9. The First Amendment: Speech that is Protected

10. The Second Amendment: Our Right to Keep and Bear Arms

11. The Fourth Amendment: Liberty and Privacy

12. The Fifth Amendment: Protecting Private Property

13. The Ninth Amendment: Affirming the People's Rights

14. The Sanctity and Dignity of Human Life

15. Respect for Our Flag: Symbol of the Constitution

16. American Sovereignty in U.S. Courts

Rather than the sections being "pro-God," from the perspective of civil rights for all Americans, several of them justify discrimination based on sexual orientation (#2, #3, #8). Others intend to protect the right of states to pass laws such as Freedom of Religion Restoration Acts (#5, #11, #8). Protecting gun rights is the purpose of #10, and #4 provides justification for Republicans cutting the budgets of federal social assistance programs. Broadly, the Platform insists that Republicans are against discrimination and for "low-income individuals" having a better chance at economic success. But the devil is in the details. Those details include the fact that the Platform is pro-business, anti-labor, anti-government, and anti-regulation, as if all that is needed to solve the social and economic problems in our country is a free market. Section #7 claims to be promoting "honest elections" when in fact it would accomplish just the opposite by endorsing state efforts to limit voting rights. Moreover, as we have already seen, the "voter fraud" the Platform calls a "poison pill" is of the Republicans' own creation.

The 2012 Republican Party Platform was, of course, a political statement, as all party platforms are. But it did provide a window into the mind and heart of Republicans that makes evangelical assertions of one party or candidate being more "Godly" than another more than a little disturbing. Yet there have become quite clever at doing so. Two weeks before the 2004 presidential election, I was visiting my mother in Lynchburg, Virginia when I saw the late Jerry Falwell show impressive skill in framing the race in this way. I was surfing through the television channels when I came upon a re-broadcast of the Thomas Road Baptist Church service held the Sunday before. Falwell was beginning his weekly political commentary that I knew from past experience was part of the Sunday service that was normally edited out for broadcast. Occasionally it was left in when Falwell wanted to make a point for the audience at large. He was talking about the upcoming election, giving his assessment of the positions of the two presidential candidates (Bush and Kerry) on moral issues. He concluded by saying, "Now I don't want you to vote Republican or Democratic. I want you to vote Christian."

He didn't have to say anything more. Based on what he had said earlier I knew exactly the candidate he thought "voting Christian" compelled me to support. I am sure the congregation did as well. It was both clever and effective, but it was also dishonest. Falwell was employing the strategy Lydia Bean argues is what most often happens in American evangelicals churches, that of "defining evangelical identity in ways that are implicitly linked to partisanship."[23]

Falwell had more skill in his subtle linking of Republican politics with Christianity or with the will of God than many evangelicals do today, but it was egregiously indefensible nonetheless in making God a member of the Republican Party. It was and is in fact a modern version of taking the Lord's name in vain. The Bible is unambiguous about God not belonging to any person, any nation, and certainly any political party. Jesus himself got into trouble in his hometown synagogue when he reminded the people that God helped non-Israelites at a time of great need in Israel (Luke 4:14–30). The congregation was so angry, in fact, that they tried to kill him. Given texts like this it is an enigma that evangelicals would ever defend their allegiance to the Republican Party or join it in the first place as if it's God's party.

Not that Republicans mind the label. The George W. Bush administration showed great skill in garnering evangelical support just after the 2004 election at a time when they were questioning his support for their issues. According to Esther Kaplan, Bush strained relations with them when he focused almost exclusively on making a case across the country for his plan to privatize Social Security. Evangelicals began to wonder if he had abandoned them after they had played a pivotal role in his reelection. But he calmed their fears, Kaplan says, by renominating seven people to the federal bench "whose records were so extreme they'd already been filibustered by the Senate." Moreover, Bush reaffirmed his support for the decision by the FDA to ban the sale of the Plan B over-the-counter emergency contraception

23. Bean, *The Politics of Evangelical Identity*, 275.

pill—the one engineered by FDA chief Mark McClellan and Advisory Board member David Hagar, an evangelical doctor adamantly opposed to abortion. He also continued funding domestic and international evangelical programs related to abstinence and AIDS treatment.[24]

One of the enigmas about the way partisan evangelicals attach the name of God or "Christian" to Republican policies and politicians is why the fact that it has often come back to bite them has not made them at all hesitate to do it. Going all the way back to the moment the House of Representatives chose to impeach President Bill Clinton for sexual indiscretions, Republican character flaws have become embarrassingly public. Illinois Representative Henry Hyde, who spearheaded the impeachment proceedings, proved himself to be chief among hypocrites when it was discovered that he had engaged in an extra-marital affair himself. Later Louisiana Republican Representative Robert Livingston was forced to resign for the same reason just as he was about to assume the position of Speaker of the House. So when the telephone number of Senator David Vitter turned up on a list of the infamous "DC Madam" in 2007, it showed how foolish evangelicals are to infer in the ways they do that God is on the side of Republicans. If that were not enough, Dennis Hastert, who became Speaker of the House after Robert Livingston's affair was made public and who presided over the House when impeachment charges brought against Clinton, was recently convicted of child molestation.

Through the years these kinds of revelations, along with evangelical "morals regulation" efforts—especially with their anti-abortion and anti-gay marriage rhetoric and actions—have not produced the kind of benefits Republicans had hoped for or expected. The percentage of Americans who view the party unfavorably, in fact, stood at 62 percent in the spring of 2016, with only 33 percent holding a favorable opinion. This compares with Democrats being viewed unfavorably by 50 percent with a favorable rating of 45 percent. In addition, while nine out of ten Democrats have a favorable opinion of their own party, only 68 percent of Republicans have a favorable view of theirs.[25] Not only do most American people not share the opinion held by evangelicals that the Republican Party is God's choice for political parties, neither do a large number of Republicans themselves. Indeed, they seem to be saying that they don't even like the image Republicans now have

24. Kaplan, *With God on Their Side*, 285.
25. Pew Research Center, "GOP's Favorability Rating Edges Lower."

as the nation's "moral police," an image evangelicals have played a major role in forging.

When the Moral Majority jumped into American politics as a partisan group of Christians, the kind of damage that would end up doing to Republicans and the nation could not have been anticipated. At the time it was seen either as a chance for the evangelicals to have a voice in shaping America's values or as a potential danger in blurring the line between church and state. As it turned out, both observations missed the mark widely. The Moral Majority and its heirs have brought chaos and division to the Republican Party, to the Congress, and to the nation. Extremism has become mainstream. Ideological rigidity has replaced pragmatic realism. Republican candidates now dance to a moralistic tune they may not even like, but cannot ignore if they hope to make it through primary challenges. Former Republican leaders who accepted compromise as the way to get important work done and who did not view Democrats as enemies are now referred to as "old line" Republicans, as if their kind has become extinct.

RELIGIOUS TESTS FOR OFFICE

What role should a candidate's faith play in the way he or she is viewed by the voting public? According to the Constitution the answer is "none." The last section of Article VI states unequivocally:

> The Senators and Representatives before mentioned, and the Members of the several State Legislatures, and all executive and judicial Officers, both of the United States and of the several States, shall be bound by Oath or Affirmation, to support this Constitution; *but no religious Test shall ever be required as a Qualification to any Office or public Trust under the United States* (italics mine).

Surveys confirm that most Americans believe in the "no religious test" mandate.[26] That is the view held by 60 percent of the nation's Democrats who say they do not want their presidential candidate to share his or her religious beliefs. The same percentage of Republicans hold just the opposite view, with 60 percent saying they do want their candidates to talk about their faith.[27] This would include an overwhelming majority of evangelicals, even those who have not made God a Republican. During the 2008

26. Jones, "Atheists, Muslims See Most Bias as Presidential Candidates."
27. Masci, "5 key findings about faith and politics in the 2016 presidential race."

presidential campaign progressive evangelical leader (with the emphasis on "progressive") Jim Wallis and his Sojourners/Call to Renewal organization sponsored a political forum for the three leading Democratic candidates (a planned forum for Republican candidates never took place). Held at George Washington University on June 4, 2007, the Democratic forum was broadcast on CNN and hosted by Soledad O'Brian. Its intentions were commendable, to provide a chance for the three candidates to have "an in-depth discussion of religion, faith and politics." Ms. O'Brian stated to the live audience and television viewers that she expected John Edwards, Hillary Clinton, and Barak Obama "to tackle some of the most important moral issues of our times."

In one respect they did. John Edwards was asked about his views on gay marriage, what he would do to bridge the gap between the rich and the poor, and what he would do to help rebuild New Orleans post-Katrina. Edwards was also asked about his personal prayer life, how prayer helped him daily, how he knew he was following "God's voice" and not his own, and what was the biggest sin he had committed (I'm not making this up!). Barack Obama was asked if he believed God took sides in war, about using the language of good and evil when talking about war, about the Israeli/Palestinian conflict, what kind of moral and political imagination he would bring to finding some real solutions to the nation's poverty rate, how he envisioned people living out their faith, about the criminal justice system and creating jobs for low income citizens, and what to do about the growing disparity between the pay CEOs receive and what their workers are paid. Hillary Clinton was asked to explain her vote for the Iraq War, about the moral responsibility she feels when she takes votes in the Senate, how her faith helped her cope with President Clinton's infidelity, what she asks God for when she prays (again, I'm not making this up), how she would help reduce abortions while being pro-choice herself, and how she would speak to the country about the need for sacrifice and restraint in regard to critical issues such as taxes, gun control, health care, and energy consumption.

At the end Wolf Blitzer reflected: "Soledad, I thought this statement from Senator Clinton and also the statements from Senator Obama and Senator Edwards on their religious values gave our viewers a little bit more insight into their background, their belief in God, and their values." She answered in several ways, at one point saying she thought Democrats were learning how to talk more freely about their faith. Then she summed up the evening by saying, "I think we're learning a lot about the values that shape the person who wants to run our country."[28] Jim Wallis remarked that he thought "a new political conversation" had begun because of the night.[29]

On one level the forum was an example of how religion gets used by all politicians. We usually associate Republican candidates with pandering to evangelicals. Donald Trump's reference to "two" Corinthians 3:17 instead of "Second Corinthians" in a speech he gave at Liberty University during the 2016 presidential campaign was a classic example.[30] But in 2008 Democrats showed they were also willing to use religion to their advantage. It's what politicians do. How many people, for example, expected John Edwards—who was involved with a woman who had given birth to his child at the very time he participated in the Forum—to say that he didn't pray daily, or that his biggest sin was adultery? How many people expected Barack Obama to say he believed God took sides in war or that moral imagination never crossed his mind when he thought about solutions to the nation's social problems or he had never really thought about how people can live out their faith in daily practice? How many expected Hillary Clinton to say faith played no decisive role in coping with her husband's infidelity, especially since in truth he had had affairs from the time they got married?

The questions were intended to begin a conversation Sojourners said would bring morality into the discussion of various issues, especially poverty, but in fact the questions asked were softballs pitched to candidates ready to say what they thought people wanted to hear. John Edwards alone proved the degree to which politicians use religion for their own selfish gain. But the most disturbing aspect of the Forum was its sanctioning of the insertion of a person's faith into politics, a point I made in an article published in *The Christian Century* soon afterwards. "I was heartened to hear that faith and prayer serve as a source of personal strength for these political leaders," I wrote, "but it completely escapes me how this affects their qualifications to be president."[31] Jim Wallis claimed the forum did no such thing. "We are not asking that faith be a qualification for office but asking how, in the case of candidates who are people of religious faith, how

28. "Democrats at the Sojourners Forum."

29. Ibid.

30. Taylor, "Citing 'Two Corinthians,' Trump Struggles To Make The Sale To Evangelicals.".

31. Linn, "On not mimicking the religious right."

their faith grounds, informs or shapes their political leadership and public policies."[32]

But what about candidates who made no claim as people of faith? To want to know how their faith shaped their political policies would have unavoidably put them on the spot not unlike allowing children to repeat the Lord's Prayer in school puts children not from a religious home on the spot. If the solution was not to include such candidates, that too would have been inappropriate. That Wallis did not understand this underscored why its prohibition is in the Constitution. What surprised me, though, was when Wallis undercut his position by referring to a communication he had received from Joel Hunter, senior pastor of Northland Church in Florida, who had participated in the Forum and who said:

> Issues will come and go, stances will sometimes change, and cir-
> cumstances will affect how a value is put into practice. But the one
> thing that seldom changes is the process of how we determine right
> from wrong. Are there certain points of reference, like the Bible,
> or the teachings of somebody, or a past mentor that the candidate
> thinks about? Are there particular people that a candidate con-
> sults? Those are all legitimate areas to explore with candidates.[33]

Perhaps they were to Reverend Hunter, but there is no way they can be justified on the basis of Article VI of the Constitution. In our form of democracy what voters need to know are the specific positions candidates hold on issues. That tells us all we need to know about their moral values. In fact, the Forum confirmed that knowing about the faith of a candidate tells nothing about who he or she really is or what he or she will do when in office. When asked who his favorite philosopher or thinker was during the Republican primary debate in Iowa, then candidate George W. Bush blurted out, "Christ . . . because he changed my life." Not to be outdone, after mentioning Lincoln and Ronald Reagan, Orrin Hatch, Senator from Utah, added, "But I bear witness to Christ, too. I really know him to be the savior of the world. And that means more to me than almost anything else I know." Evangelical candidate Gary Bauer quoted Scripture in naming Christ as his favorite political thinker, adding, "If America's in trouble in the next century, it will be because we forgot what he taught us."[34]

---

32. Wallis, "Principled, not partisan, politics."

33. Ibid.

34. Buttry, "Candidates focus on Christian beliefs."

These comments not only show the impact of evangelicals on the Republican Party as each candidate felt the need to outdo the other about their personal faith, but George Bush proved as president that faith played no role in the moral decisions about war and torture that he made. He might have followed former New Jersey Senator Bill Bradley's example when he persistently refused to say anything during his brief 2000 presidential nomination campaign about his faith. To him it was a private matter not subject to public discussion or debate. Catholic scholar and priest Andrew Greeley wrote about Bradley's position in an article that could have saved the Sojourner Forum from making the mistake it did.

> The president's private life is no one's business save his own, unless he clearly violates the law. The public has the right to know, it will be argued. Funny, I don't hear any noisy public clamor to learn about how Bradley relates to God. The public seems much more interested in what he proposes to do about health care and gun control and how he intends to sustain the present happy condition of the economy. I suspect many of the public are not a little put off by the pieties the various candidates are slinging around . . . . We tend to suspect public officials who are too obvious, not to say sanctimonious, about their faith and their virtues.

Then, in his typically humorous way, Greeley spoke truth as was his habit:

> St. Teresa of Avila once remarked she would rather have a wise confessor than a holy one. I'd vote for a wise president in preference to a holy one or one who claims to be holy. She also said that from silly devotions and sour faced saints, libera nos domine —deliver us O Lord! I'll vote for that. I'd also vote for a candidate —if he were not an ex-Knick—who said to the American people, "You have a claim on me to perform well at my job. I'll do my best. However, you have no right to poke your noses around into what I'm doing, what I think or how I pray when I'm not on the job."[35]

That said, it is incomprehensible that eight states—Arkansas, Maryland, Mississippi, North Carolina, Pennsylvania, South Carolina, Tennessee, and Texas—currently have laws on the books declaring that a person who does not profess belief in God cannot hold public office. Were they ever to be enforced, they would certainly be found unconstitutional, but the fact that they are there at all serves as a warning to how easy it is for us

---

35. Greeley, "Senator Bradley's Religion."

as a people to violate the beliefs that are core to having the form of democracy we have. What matters in elections is where candidates stand on the issues, not their professed religious beliefs. Would that evangelicals might someday agree.

COLLATERAL DAMAGE

"The law of unintended consequences, often cited but rarely defined," writes Rob Norton, former editor of *Fortune* magazine, "is that actions of people—and especially of government—always have effects that are unanticipated or unintended."[36] While discussions of the law of unintended consequences are most often related to economics, I suggest that it applies quite accurately to evangelical efforts at "morals regulation," past and present. Our nation's history is replete with examples to support my claim.

The criminalization of homosexuality is at the top of the list. Before the 2004 Supreme Court ruling that struck down a Texas anti-sodomy law, such laws were common across the country. Ten states still have them, but no judge would sentence a person to jail for being a homosexual. Nor would responsible prosecutors bring such charges, as was the case when police conducted a raid in East Baton Rouge, Louisiana in 2013. They arrested gay men on the basis of the state's antiquated anti-sodomy law, but the district attorney refused to prosecute. In his view the anti-sodomy law was unenforceable. Yet Republican legislators refused to appeal the law when Democratic Senator Patricia Smith submitted a bill to that effect. Gene Mills, president of the evangelical Louisiana Family Forum, remarked after the vote that the bill was "not a Louisiana value."[37] Another way of putting what he said might be to say that anyone not heterosexual is of no value in the state of Louisiana. Such is the thinking of many evangelicals.

One of the truly tragic consequences of "morals regulation" is that so many other concerns demanding attention go unnoticed because people have limited time, energy, and resources to attend to everything. Louisiana under former evangelical Bobby Jindal is a telling example. Jindal, a Hindu convert to Protestant Christianity first and then Catholicism later, said often during his tenure as governor that "the single most important time in my life is the moment that I found Jesus Christ." Thus, Jindal governed as an evangelical first and a secular head of state second. He was a strong

36. Norton, "Unintended Consequences."

37. *USA Today*, "12 states still ban sodomy a decade after court ruling."

advocate for a constitutional amendment against same-sex marriage. He initiated TRAP laws in Louisiana to limit abortion access. When the legislature failed to pass a religious freedom law Jindal issued what he called a "marriage and conscience" executive order that would allow businesses not to serve same-sex couples. He also fought raising taxes and spearheaded the largest tax cut in the state's history. He produced austere budgets that left education officials begging for more funding and social programs being cut drastically. He also refused to expand Medicaid that would have provided health insurance to thousands of low-income Louisianans, but gave away tax breaks to large corporations that didn't need them.

Meanwhile the state of Louisiana was going broke. When Jindal left office he left behind a $1.6 billion deficit. Jindal claimed it was the drop in oil prices that caused the state's financial troubles, but even the *American Conservative* online carried a story that stated bluntly that what broke Louisiana's economy was "the fiscal policy pushed by the Jindal administration and backed by the State Legislature."[38] In 2016 Moody's Investors Service downgraded Louisiana's credit rating, making it more expensive for the state to borrow money to keep operating. Current Democratic Governor John Bel Edwards calls Jindal "the most irresponsible governor who has ever governed Louisiana."[39]

It seems almost generous to suggest that Bobby Jindal's evangelical faith led him to be much more focused on "morals regulations" than he was on improving the lives of the people of his state. But he was and he is not alone. The same thing could be said of Kansas Republican Governor Sam Brownback and the Republican-controlled state legislature. The credit rating for that state has also been lowered, and the state is running a deficit in the billions because of tax policies that cut taxes that did not result in increased revenue. Meanwhile Kansas is the premier example of "morals regulation" by the state, embodied in ways seen nowhere else in the person of former state Attorney General Phil Kline. So egregious were his actions that he had his license to practice law indefinitely suspended by the Kansas Supreme Court for professional misconduct during his tenure as Attorney general and as the Johnson County district attorney.

In the latter instance, Kline was in charge of investigating the murder of Dr. George Tiller, who was killed because he performed abortions. Kline

38. Dreher, "How Bobby Jindal Wrecked Louisiana."

39. Pierce, "Bobby Jindal Is Going Around Offering Advice While the State He Just Left Falls Apart."

chose instead to accuse Planned Parenthood and the deceased Tiller of violating state abortion law and covering for pedophiles by not reporting pregnancies of underage girls, and tried to have Planned Parenthood turn over the medical records of former patients to prove his case. This led to a 107-count criminal indictment that was later dismissed by the current district attorney. Kline's suspension was based in part on the following findings during his Johnson County tenure:

> The court found Friday that when he was attorney general, Kline committed misconduct by instructing members of his staff to attach sealed documents to a publicly filed document in violation of a Supreme Court order. He also told staff to file a court pleading that contained misleading information.
>
> The court further found that as Johnson County district attorney, Kline failed to properly advise members of a grand jury about Kansas law and sought to enforce a grand jury subpoena against the grand jury's wishes.
>
> It also found that Kline gave false testimony to a judge and made "false and misleading" statements to the Supreme Court about the handling of patient records obtained during the criminal investigations. He also did not correct a misstatement to the state's disciplinary administrator regarding the storage of patient records.[40]

Another unintended consequence states have faced as legislators have spent their time enacting morality laws and officials like Kline have pursued personal vendettas is the incredible financial burden these actions have created for states. Every TRAP law, every religious freedom restoration law, every bill that favors Christianity over other religions, every effort of an attorney general or secretary of state to play loose with the nation's Constitution becomes a court battle that costs taxpayers money. Kline himself cost Kansas millions of dollars because of the bogus lawsuits he filed against Planned Parenthood, doctors, and other clinics that provided abortion services. But Kansas was hardly alone in wasteful morality spending. In 2014 the state of Alaska spent over $100,000 defending its anti-gay marriage law at a time when it was facing a $3 billion deficit.[41] In August of 2015 the state of Idaho paid out nearly $1 million in its defense of three lawsuits involving a same-sex marriage case, its defense of an anti-abortion law that was ruled unconstitutional, and the Occupy Boise case in which

40. Rizzo, "Phil Kline is indefinitely suspended from practicing law." .

41. Caldwell, "Cost to state of defending same-sex marriage lawsuit tops $100,000."

the state sought to restrict camping and demonstrations around the state capitol.[42] South Dakota spent more than $750,000 defending its unconstitutional anti-abortion law in 2011. Texas spent $650,000 trying to roll back abortion rights.[43] The state of Utah spent more than $1 million defending its anti-abortion laws in the 1990s.[44]

These are only a few of the states that have spent millions and millions of dollars defending "morals regulation" laws, all of which even supporters know have little chance of surviving a constitutional challenge. This financial burden evangelicals place on the citizens of states across the country deserves more attention than it has received. But the costs don't stop with court and attorney fees. Because of the new law, for example, that blocks cities from enacting LGBT nondiscrimination protections and mandates that transgender people use the wrong bathrooms for their gender identities, North Carolina has lost PayPal's global operations center planned for Charlotte. The company said that "the new law perpetuates discrimination and it violates the values and principles that are at the core of PayPal's mission and culture."[45] The economic impact of this loss to the city is estimated to be in the billions over time, including more than 400 new jobs.

When Indiana passed a similar law last year, nine CEOs of the state's major corporations—Eli Lilly and Co., Anthem, Indiana University Health, Angie's List, Emmis Communications, Roche Diagnostics, Dow Agro Sciences, Cummins Engine, and Cook Group—signed a letter that was made public calling on then-Governor Mike Pence to take steps to ensure the law did not provide legal support for discrimination against LGBT persons. Business reaction to these kinds of laws is why Georgia Governor Nathan Deal vetoed one his legislature passed. After the era of civil rights, Atlanta businesses promoted the slogan, "The City Too Busy To Hate." After the governor's veto, William Pate, head of the Atlanta Convention and Visitors Bureau commented, "I think his decision is really going to sustain Georgia's position as the No. 1 state in which to do business."[46]

Businesses urging Republicans not to enact "morals regulation" bills is a scenario we are not accustomed to seeing in America, but this is the point we have reached because of extremism spawned and nurtured by

42. Russell, "Idaho to pay nearly $1M to plaintiffs for attorney fees in three cases."
43. Coutts, "Texas Spends Nearly $650,000 Defending Anti-Choice Laws."
44. Adams, "New Utah AG: Cost to defend same-sex marriage ban worthwhile."
45. Ford, "North Carolina Just Lost 400 Jobs Because Of Its Anti-LGBT Law."
46. Geewax, "Atlanta Businesses Again Lead Push Against Social Conservatives."

evangelicals and their political partisanship. Foolish decisions affect everyone, not just the few. We may not be fighting in the streets, but the collateral damage in the culture war is very real.

FOSTERING ANTI-MUSLIM SENTIMENT

In September 2016, a Pew Research Center survey found that 82 percent of Republicans are "very concerned" about the rise of Islamic extremism in the world, compared to 60 percent of political independents and 51 percent of Democrats. Similarly, two-thirds of Republicans (67 percent) say that Islam is more likely than other religions to encourage violence among its believers, compared to 47 percent of independents and 42 percent of Democrats.

These results reflect the fact that rank and file evangelicals are woefully uninformed about the views of Muslims around the world. A 2015 survey found that 79 percent of Indonesians (the largest population of Muslims anywhere) have an unfavorable opinion of ISIS. It also found that 94 percent of Jordanians feel the same way, as do 97 percent of Muslims living in Israel, 84 percent living in Palestinian territories, 73 percent in Turkey, 66 percent in Nigeria, and 60 percent in Senegal. Pakistan had the lowest unfavorable opinion of ISIS at 28 percent, with the majority—62 percent—having no opinion at all. But in no country in the survey did ISIS have more than a 15 percent favorable rating.[47]

Not only does ISIS have little support among most Muslims, Islamic scholars and teachers have repeated statements condemning ISIS for misrepresenting genuine Islamic values and teachings. Yet evangelical Republicans dismiss surveys and statements by Muslims around the world as if they are speaking untruths or reflect naïveté about the threat Islam poses. Such attitudes are encouraged by political candidates who urge the nation's police forces to step up patrolling in Muslim neighborhoods. "We need to empower law enforcement to patrol and secure Muslim neighborhoods before they become radicalized," is how one candidate put it, adding that the nation can "no longer afford 'political correctness.'"[48] In addition, 59 percent of Republicans say they support the suggestion by another candidate

47. Poushter, "In nations with significant Muslim populations, much disdain for ISIS."

48. Diamond, "Ted Cruz: Police need to 'patrol and secure' Muslim neighborhoods."

that the government ban Muslims who are not American citizens from entering the country.[49]

The results of all these surveys show that anti-Muslim sentiment among Republicans in general and evangelicals in particular is based on fear more than facts. Illustrative of how irrational fear can become, since 9/11 there have been several efforts to enact anti-Sharia laws in various Republican-controlled legislatures, According to a report released by the Council on American-Islamic Relations in 2013, during the two years before "78 bills or amendments aimed at interfering with Islamic religious practices or vilifying Islam were considered in 31 states and the US Congress. Sixty-two of these bills contained language that was extracted from Islamophobe David Yerushalmi's American Laws for American Courts (ALAC) model for legislation proposals."[50] Yerushalmi, a Hasidic Jew, lawyer, political activist, and co-founder of the American Freedom Law Center is the driving force behind the anti-Sharia movement in the United States.

Efforts like this ignore the fact that Article VI, Clause 2 of the Constitution states plainly and succinctly: "This Constitution . . . shall be the supreme law of the land; and the judges in every state shall be bound thereby." There can be no substitute law for the Constitution as any attempt to enact Sharia Law, the Ten Commandments, or the Sermon of the Mount would represent. More than that, the First Amendment prohibits Congress or any other body from making any law "respecting an establishment of religion." Given these constitutional facts, the political motivation of anti-Sharia laws becomes obvious. They do not address a real threat. They are a tool for people like David Yerushalmi who promote anti-Islamic feelings within the US in order to strengthen the pro-Israel political lobby. That is why evangelical lobbies and legislators are willing to join in Yerishalmi's campaign.

The seriousness of evangelical anti-Muslim rhetoric and legislative efforts cannot be overstated. Its context is a world with approximately 3.2 billion Christians and approximately 1.6 billion Muslims. Together we make up almost two-thirds of the world's population. It is not difficult to see that good relations between these two dominant religions will either help the cause of world peace or harm it. The United States cannot afford to be seen by the Muslim world as its archenemy. Most sensible political leaders understand that danger, but there are enough radicals in Congress and in state

49. Clement, "Republicans embrace Trump's ban on Muslims while most others reject it."

50. *A Brief Overview of the Pervasiveness of Anti-Islam Legislation.*

legislatures to convince Muslims here and around the world that there are strong anti-Muslim advocates weighing in on US foreign policy.

Dr. John Esposito, Georgetown Professor of Religion and International Affairs, says a major problem with policy makers in Washington is "that they have largely treated political Islam as a global threat similar to the way that Communism was perceived." He goes on to say they moved from "an ill-informed, broad-brush, and paranoid approach personified by Senator Joseph McCarthy in the 1950s to more nuanced, pragmatic, and reasonable policies that led to the establishment of relations with China in the 1970s." This, he argues, is what the US must now do in regard to "political Islam."

"Is the primary cause of radicalism and anti-Westernism," he asks, "especially anti-Americanism, extremist theology or simply the policies of many Muslim and Western governments? A new Gallup World Study overwhelmingly suggests the latter." The survey asked respondents if they thought the 9/11 attacks on the US were justified. Only 7 percent said they were 'completely' justified and expressed strong criticism of the United States. Among those who believe that 9/11 was not justified, 40 percent were pro-U.S., and 60 percent viewed the U.S. favorably." Further, Esposito notes,

> When asked what they admired most about the West, both extremists and moderates had the identical top three spontaneous responses: (1) technology; (2) the West's value system, hard work, self-responsibility, rule of law, and cooperation; and (3) its fair political systems, democracy, respect for human rights, freedom of speech, and gender equality. A significantly higher percent of potential extremists than moderates (50 percent versus 35 percent) believe that "moving towards greater governmental democracy" will foster progress in the Arab/Muslim world. Potential extremists believe even more strongly than moderates (58 percent versus 45 percent) that Arab/Muslim nations are eager to have better relations with the West. Finally, no significant difference exists between the percentage of potential extremists and moderates who said "better relations with the West concerns me a lot."[51]

But perhaps the wisdom of one our own children might open evangelical eyes to the damage they are doing. Twelve-year-old Muslim-American Zara Ahsan recently met Takako "Kit" Nishiura, a woman who was imprisoned in the US internment camps during WWII when she was about

51. Esposito, "It's The Policy Stupid: Political Islam and US Foreign Policy."

Zara's age. Reflecting on the conversation she had with Takako, Zara wrote the following:

> I am a sixth grader, born and bred in the Bay Area. My friends hail from a variety of backgrounds, and like a lot of them, I like music, drama and sports. Although they have many of the same interests as I do, they speak different languages, eat different foods and voice their own opinions. We get on really well and I don't know what I'd do without them.
>
> Every day at school, we recite the Pledge of Allegiance and we talk about how America is the home of the free, with liberty and justice for all. I've always believed that I was lucky to live in the best country in the world because of all the progress we have made, the power of democracy, and how great our nation is. What I was not aware of, is that we don't always treat our own people very well, and sometimes we completely abandon liberty and justice for some for our own convenience.
>
> Our ideals are amazing, but what happened to the Japanese-Americans during World War II shows that we don't always honor our ideals. Nowadays, similarly derogatory language is being directed against Muslims. Me and many other young Americans are worried about what will happen if our freedom is taken away and we are treated the same as the Japanese Americans during that shameful time. For all the progress that America has made, would history repeat itself?[52]

Out of the mouths of babes. But will evangelicals listen? Until they do they will continue to spew forth hatred and spread fear in the name of God and in the name of being Christian. For this reason our nation cannot afford to tolerate evangelicalism as just another religion that has the right to do whatever it chooses to say and do. Groups that sow discord and preach prejudice are guilty of trying to create a social unrest that tears a nation apart. When such a group claims to be religious, their rhetoric and behavior is all the more heinous. Evangelical partisans don't deserve our tolerance, they deserve our scorn.

DISMISSING (OR DISSING) THE CONSTITUTION

Whenever evangelicals get Republican politicians to do their moral bidding more often than not the results are laws passed that intentionally challenge

---

52. Mathias, "An American Muslim Kid's Message To Her Country."

or try to circumvent the US Constitution. They justify what they do by insisting that all laws are morally based and, thus, their efforts to regulate morality are constitutional:

> All laws, whether prescriptive or prohibitive, legislate morality. All laws, regardless of their content or their intent, arise from a system of values, from a belief that some things are right and others wrong, that some things are good and others bad, that some things are better and others worse. In the formulation and enforcement of law, the question is never whether or not morality will be legislated, but which one.[53]

Morally based or not, though, the reality about any law passed is that it must meet constitutional standards. Fully aware that the establishment of a nation involved morality in order for there to be order, freedom, and justice, our founders nonetheless forged a Constitution that embodies universal values that transcend a single religious tradition. Throughout this book I have noted numerous survey results that confirm that most Americans do not share evangelical positions on most moral issues. In that context it would seem reasonable to expect evangelicals to support the good intentions of the majority of Americans by supporting laws on which most of us can agree. Imposing the will of the minority on the majority is a strategy doomed to failure. Worse, it causes unrest and conflict. Perhaps, though, that is the real intention of evangelicals.

At the very least their rejection of compromise makes the question of motives all the more important as we look to the future. At the moment Republicans are becoming marginalized. They have won the nationwide popular vote for president once in the last twenty-eight years. Whatever political power they have exists because of gerrymandering that changes every ten years. This means the constant in Republican politics for a generation has been losing national elections. Voters are saying in various ways to Republicans that they know government cannot function without compromise. When Republicans accused President Obama of refusing to negotiate the facts suggested they must have been trying to make people laugh to alleviate some tension. Senator Elizabeth Warren released a report in June of 2016 (available on the Internet) detailing Republican obstructionism.[54] That she is a Democrat does not change the fact that she is also a former college professor of law and knows reports of this nature must con-

53. Bauman, "Law and Morality."
54. Warren, "Going to Extremes."

tain reliable statistics to be credible. They do in these instances, confirming the characterization of Republican behavior over the last seven years in the report's title, "Going to Extremes." The only reason for the "extremes" to which they have gone is the refusal to compromise. Common sense says that when it's my way or no way, no way prevails. Republicans not only want to control the government—they want to *own* it.

There is no future for the party with that attitude, as E. J. Dionne contends. Believing the nation needs a strong and vibrant Republican Party, he says for that to happen Republicans will have to do the following:

> They will have to accept in practice what many acknowledge in theory: that to be successful and grow, a market economy requires a rather large government and a significant commitment to social insurance. They certainly do not have to embrace all cultural change uncritically, but they will need to accept its inevitability if they wish to preserve what is most valuable in our national tradition. And they would do well to acknowledge that the business of running a competent government in a racially and culturally diverse nation requires tolerance and compromise.[55]

He then suggests: "conservatives must recover the idea that extremism in the pursuit of their political goals is a vice, and remember that moderation in approaching problems of governing is a virtue.[56]

That, in fact, is the only way to govern. In the past, political leaders have overcome differences to accomplish great things. Today, they cannot overcome differences at all to accomplish even the smallest of tasks. Evangelical partisanship has helped to make it this way the same way its theological claims have shut the door to any other Christian perspectives. They do not believe in working with people whose views are different from their own. That is the epitome of bad politics that is undermining our way of life.

A BETTER WAY FORWARD

One of the co-founders of the Moral Majority in 1979 was political consultant Paul Weyrich. In fact, he is the person who coined the term "Moral Majority." Weyrich had founded the conservative think tank The Heritage Foundation in 1973, but he wanted to go after the evangelical vote. His strategy was to politicize evangelicals and build a Republican constituency.

55. Dionne, *Why the Right Went Wrong*, 25.
56. Ibid.

That is what happened when the Moral Majority was formed. From that point to now various evangelical political organizations have risen to become major players in the Republican Party. The number is staggering. Below is a list I was able to compile from various sources.

> First Liberty Institute
>
> Christian News
>
> Association for Biblical Higher Education
>
> Aglow International (Women Aglow)
>
> Alliance of Confessing Evangelicals
>
> American Family Association
>
> American Scientific Affiliation
>
> Association of Christian Schools International
>
> Association of Gospel Rescue Missions
>
> Bibles For the World
>
> Billy Graham Evangelistic Association (BGEA)
>
> Campus Crusade for Christ International
>
> Christian Broadcasting Network (CBN)
>
> Christian Camping International
>
> Christian Coalition
>
> Christian Stewardship Association
>
> Christianity Today Inc.
>
> Compassion International
>
> Concerned Women For America
>
> Council for Christian Colleges and Universities
>
> Crown Financial Ministries (Christian Financial Concepts)
>
> Evangelical Council for Financial Accountability
>
> Evangelicals For Social Action
>
> Faith and Freedom Coalition
>
> Family Research Council (Gary Bauer, Tony Perkins)
>
> Fellowship of Christian Athletes
>
> Focus on the Family (James Dobson)
>
> Full Gospel Businessman's Fellowship International
>
> Gospel Music Association
>
> Grace to You (John MacArthur)
>
> Harvest Crusades (Greg Laurie)
>
> Intercristo

Inter-Varsity Christian Fellowship (USA)

Jews For Jesus

Luis Palau Evangelistic Association

Liberty Council

MAP International

Ministry Watch

National Association of Evangelicals (NAE)

National Religious Broadcasters (NRB)

Navigators

Prison Fellowship (Charles Colson)

Promise Keepers

Samaritan's Purse (Franklin Graham)

World Vision

Youth for Christ

Young Life

Youth With a Mission (YWAM)

This list tells the story of a nationwide evangelical effort to engage in partisan politics, influence public policy, and alter the course of American political history. They have a strong argument for claiming they have done just that. But the *direction* of that change is what matters, and in that regard the story I have sought to tell contains overwhelming evidence that evangelicals have done far more harm than good. That said, there are a few voices among Republicans that are less strident and much more thoughtful about what our nation can do to find its way again. They know that at this point whoever is president will face the same stalemated Congress President Obama lived with for eight years. Yet they also believe Republicans who bear the lion's share of responsibility for the ways things are can bring about needed change. One group, "Religion & Politics, Fit For Polite Company," founded and led by former Republican Senator John Danforth of Missouri, has the kind of credibility to help point a new direction for the Republican Party. The purpose statement of Religion & Politics describes the kind of political culture it believes Republicans need to help the Congress recover:

> We feature articles from scholars and journalists who proceed from a single premise: that for better and for worse, religion and politics converge, clash, and shape public life. These intersections happen everywhere, from our homes to our courts, from the

statehouse to the schoolhouse, in the lab and on the battlefield. We strive to publish a range of views, rather than promoting a specific political perspective. We honor frank and respectful debate. We inform these discussions by taking the long view, providing historical context, critical analysis, and thorough research with compelling writing.[57]

A commitment to discuss religion and politics in the context of "frank and respectful debate" may be all that is needed to tame the extremism that is so dominant in American politics at the moment. That is because it will remind us from whence we have come, to the realization that the laws of our land at the state and local levels must be consistent with the rights guaranteed by the Constitution and are applied equally regardless of race, creed, color, nationality, or sexual orientation. It is not the job of the judiciary to make rulings based on personal bias. It is not the job of members of Congress or the President to pass laws that violate the letter or the spirit of the Constitution. It is not the job of state legislatures and governors to figure out legal ways to circumvent the intent and content of federal laws or the rulings of the Supreme Court. It is not the job of citizens to want any branch of government to favor its beliefs over all others. It is, rather, incumbent upon us to want the best for all and to sacrifice whenever that means making amends for wrongs done to others. We are a people who tolerate extremism, but seldom do we embrace it, and never for an extended period of time.

Another voice among Republicans similar to John Danforth's is David Gergen, a Republican advisor to both Republican and Democratic presidents and currently Professor of Public Service and co-director of the Center for Public Leadership at the Harvard Kennedy School. In 2016 he challenged the graduating class at Elon University in North Carolina to resist the temptation to stand on the sidelines of American political life and choose instead to get involved. A native of Carolina himself, Gergen expressed alarm at the political climate the Republican-dominated legislature there had created. "Enough is enough," he said. "For those of us who have stayed on the sidelines, it is time to stand up and be counted. It is time to raise our voices against this darkness. Indeed, it is time for fellow citizens of all stripes—white and black; young and old; native and newcomer; men,

57. Danforth, Religion & Politics.

women and people of chosen gender—everyone—to join forces and preserve the best of who we are as a people."[58]

He proceeded to tell of past North Carolina leaders who stood up for a New South that honored the rights of all while listening and respecting voices of disagreement. They were leaders who he described as believing in moderation, reaching across the aisle, building consensus, and the importance of good will. "Then suddenly," he declared, "without warning, dark clouds arrived. The moderation that characterized our state—the belief among Republicans and Democrats that we are all in this together—gave way to a new, angrier, extremist politics." He described the current North Carolina Republican leadership and their supporters as those who "want to go back, far back to a darker time," ending with a stirring challenge:

> May I plead with you: please don't stay on the sidelines as America struggles to find the best path forward. Come off the bench and get into the arena. You will find that many will disagree with you, just as many here will have disagreed with me. But don't let your disagreements make them your enemies. Find common ground, work hard to respect the views of others. You will get knocked down and there will be severe disappointments. Embrace the fact that change is hard. But know this: if you pour your heart and soul into rebuilding a better state and nation, you will look back one day and find an inner satisfaction, a pride that you answered the call to service and leadership.[59]

Gergen's challenge to those graduates should speak to all of us who want to see our nation reject extremist voices that advocate policies and laws that will continue to divide us against one another. In these times sitting on the sidelines is not an option. The very political system we believe in and cherish is under assault by various forces, including those who think they are doing the work of God.

58. Anderson, "'Enough is Enough.'"
59. Ibid.

5

WHY PARTISAN EVANGELICALISM
IS BAD RELIGION

BAD RELIGION IS SOMETHING people know intuitively, but cannot always define. For this reason it often means different things to different people. Evangelicals might define "bad religion" as a set of beliefs that do not conform to what they believe are the essentials of the Christian faith. Others might define "bad religion" as consisting of beliefs evangelicals insist are essential. It is a problem for every religion because within every faith tradition people not only believe different things, but assign different degrees of importance to those beliefs. Usually their beliefs are core, while the beliefs of others are tangential.

One way to cope with the subjectivity endemic to assessing good and bad religion is to follow the counsel of Jesus as he spoke about how to know a true prophet from a false one: "You will know them by their fruits" (Matt 7:20). Using this measure of judgment, the previous chapters have noted numerous examples of the "bad" fruit American evangelicalism has been producing, especially because of its Republican partisanship. It's not that evangelicals are bad people. It's the fact that what good people often believe can and does have extremely bad consequences. The victims of the tragic shooting at a gay night club in Orlando, Florida on June 12, 2016 found that out in the worst way. Many influences turned Omar Mateen into who he was before he did such a deed, one of which was a radical version of Islam that may have fed his homophobia.

Radicalism happens in any religion, especially when its members believe that their way is the only way, as is the case with both Islam and

Christianity. Radical Christianity is taught and preached in evangelical churches across the country every Sunday. Just after the Orlando shooting Pastor Stephen L. Anderson of Faithful Word Baptist Church in Tempe, Arizona used radical speech in his response:

> Now let me just be real clear: I've never advocated for violence. I don't believe in, you know, taking the law into our own hands. I would never go in and shoot up a gay bar—so-called. I don't believe it's right for us to just be a vigilante . . . . But I will say this: The Bible says that homosexuals should be put to death, in Leviticus 20:13. Obviously, it's not right for somebody to just, you know, shoot up the place, because that's not going through the proper channels. But these people all should have been killed, anyway, but they should have been killed through the proper channels, as in they should have been executed by a righteous government that would have tried them, convicted them, and saw them executed. Because, in Leviticus 20:13, God's perfect law, he put the death penalty on murder, and he also put the death penalty on homosexuality. That's what the Bible says, plain and simple.[1]

Anderson is only one example of the bad religion evangelical preachers espoused in their reaction to Orlando. Baptist Pastor Roger Jimenez told his congregation in Sacramento, California that Christians "shouldn't be mourning the death of 50 sodomites. People say, like: 'Well, aren't you sad that 50 sodomites died?' Here's the problem with that. It's like the equivalent of asking me—what if you asked me: 'Hey, are you sad that 50 pedophiles were killed today?' Um, no, I think that's great. I think that helps society. You know, I think Orlando, Florida, is a little safer tonight." He then added, "I wish the government would round them all up, put them up against a firing wall, put a firing squad in front of them, and blow their brains out."[2]

Anti-gay pastor Donnie Romero of Stedfast Baptist Church in Fort Worth, Texas who had told his congregation that he agreed "100 percent" with what Jimenez had said suggested in a midweek sermon that members of his church would be prepared to shoot LGBT activists if they protested outside his church building on Sunday. "There are people here who have guns, and they're going to protect the building . . . . In our church, we have men that are armed. They are permitted, they are armed, and they know

---

1. Prager, "Christian Pastor Calls Orlando Massacre 'Good News' Because 50 'F*ggots' Died."

2. Bever, "Pastor refuses to mourn Orlando victims."

how to shoot, and they know how to protect themselves, and that's a line of defense."[3]

These vile words coming from these particular evangelical preachers most assuredly did not represent the way many—in fact, most—evangelicals reacted to the Orlando tragedy. Nonetheless, too often such vileness is tolerated by other evangelicals as if freedom of religion gives ministers of this temperament the right to speak for God. That is irresponsible. In the strongest terms possible condemnation of such statements should come from the evangelical community whenever extremists like this get in the news. Having the right to say something doesn't make it morally right, and evangelicals should be willing to say so unequivocally.

PERILS OF AN UNEDUCATED CLERGY

Evangelical extremism such as we see in the comments above points to a larger problem that exists in evangelical circles. It is the lack of educational standards for clergy. The emergence of what is called "the prosperity gospel," an oxymoron if there ever was one, is symptomatic of the impact the lack of education has had. It insists that Jesus wants his followers to prosper financially. It's God's icing on a salvation cake. "Unlike the moral majority leaders of the past 30 years," writer Elizabeth Dias says, "prosperity preachers don't just want Americans to be saved. They want them to be successful."[4]

Instead of arising from the teachings of Jesus, though, his words are used to bless good old fashioned American materialism. It is truly astonishing that Jesus' name would be associated with material prosperity, but that is what happens when ill-informed ministers preach that material prosperity is the way to measure the success God wants you to have. Journalist Sarah Posner exposes them for the frauds they are in her book, *God's Profits: Faith, Fraud, and the Republican Crusade for Values Voters*. They preach that believers are given revelation and don't need reason, she says. They have the right to divine health and to divine wealth. Tithes and offerings demonstrate a congregant's faith in God. Poverty is a sign of lack of faith in God to provide.[5] It all makes sense within the universe that prosper-

3. Wright, "'Death to Gays' Pastor Donnie Romero Threatens Violence Against LGBT Protesters."

4. Dias, "Donald Trump's Prosperity Preachers."

5. Posner, *God's Profits*, 14.

ity preachers create and unsuspecting parishioners embrace with willing hearts. Her book is one story after another of the top prosperity preachers, men and women, who use religion to get rich. The saddest part is that it is working.

Joel Osteen, perhaps the most prominent of the prosperity gospel preachers, has turned "ministry" into a successful business that has made him a very wealthy man. With his personal worth estimated to be around $40 million, not including his $10 million home, he is a major financial star by American standards. He also has political power. When he completed the $75 million renovation of the Houston Compaq Sports Center both former Republican Texas Governor Rick Perry and former Democratic Speaker of the House Nancy Pelosi attended the dedication service.

Osteen is hardly alone, though, in reaping the financial reward for preaching American prosperity in the name of Jesus. Rod Parsley persuaded his congregation to provide him with his own jet so he could travel the country in the name of Jesus. T. D. Jakes, using the financial services of Joel Osteen's brother, Justin, has learned how to negotiate his compensation package to his considerable advantage. These three are major prosperity gospel stars, but as Posner's book shows, the number of others who have "proven" God is blessing them through financial success are legion.

Yet the majority of these ministers have not been theologically trained in the way Catholic priests and mainline Protestant clergy are before they can be ordained. One is a college dropout (from Oral Roberts University), one holds a BA in ministry from Ohio Christian University (formerly Circleville Bible College), a non-credited Bible college whose sole mission is to produce Christian preachers and missionaries, and another received multiple degrees through correspondence courses. Jerry Falwell Sr. graduated from Baptist Bible College in Springfield, Missouri, which had no accreditation when he attended. In fact it had only been in existence a few years (founded in 1950) at the time of his enrollment. When compared to mainline seminary education these schools teach at a Sunday school level. Absent is any serious attention to the historical critical method of biblical hermeneutics, the development of skills for textual and word study, a proficient level of biblical languages, or exposure to the history of Christian theology. There is no experience of informal debates among faculty and students on various biblical texts or theological arguments that are commonplace in seminaries. These schools avoid such practices for the simple reason that diversity of biblical and theological views is frowned upon.

Many evangelical colleges and seminaries—Southern Baptist, South-western Baptist, and Westminster. to name three prominent examples—require faculty to sign pledges of faith from which they cannot deviate without consequences. Larycia Hawkins, an Associate Professor of Political Science at academically respected Wheaton College, was disciplined and eventually agreed to vacate her position in 2016 because of a comment she made that Muslims and Christians worshipped the same God. Seeking to clarify its position, the college administration issued a statement that said: "As they participate in various causes, it is essential that faculty and staff engage in and speak about public issues in ways that faithfully represent the College's evangelical Statement of Faith."[6] Hawkins is currently serving as a visiting faculty fellow at the University of Virginia.

In 2008 the Board of Trustees at Westminster Theological Seminary suspended Professor Peter Enns from teaching because of the views he expressed in his book *Inspiration and Incarnation?*, published three years before. The book challenged evangelical beliefs regarding the inerrancy of Scripture, the meaning of divine inspiration, and the historical reliability of texts such as the creation stories in Genesis. While it caused no stir among mainline faculty, students, and trustees, it became a flash point of controversy in evangelical circles that eventually led to Enns losing his position. The message this action sent was clear. There are limits to theological study in the evangelical theological community. In short, doctrine and belief have a more important place than the pursuit of truth. What this does is encourage an attitude of caution and outright suspicion of knowledge in preparing people for ministry. In this kind of environment people who feel "called" to preach jump into it without any concern about what they don't know. They must get about the business of saving the world. That is what led to evangelicalism ordaining eleven-year-old Ezekiel Stoddard.

This child is described as "an ordained minister with unshakeable faith and extraordinary charisma."[7] In a YouTube video of him he appears to be a precocious child, perhaps a prodigy, as his family believes. He is no doubt sincere as are the adults around him. But his story is a snapshot of the appalling disregard for education that exists in evangelicalism. An eleven-year-old child is a child, period. He may be a wonderful, sincere, inspirational child, but he is a child nonetheless, and as such could not possess

6. Hauserdec, "Wheaton College Professor Is Put on Leave After Remarks Supporting Muslims." See also www.wheaton.edu.

7. YouTube, "Is This Young Boy the Future of Religion?

the experience, insight, or knowledge required to assume responsibility for preaching. He could be a very smart child, but he has no business doing what he is doing. Education is not about the ability to think. It is about using that ability to acquire knowledge you cannot possess until you spend the time learning it. Ezekiel Stoddard may one day do what he should and study for ministry, but until that time he should be the child he is. Yet every adult around him speaks admiringly of his "special gift" as if that has made education unnecessary.

This issue is not about the ability of evangelicals to do serious theological work. I know firsthand that Jerry Falwell Sr. was a very smart man, finishing at the top of his high school class, and attended an accredited private college in Virginia before attending Bible college. He was quite capable of doing high-level academic study. He just didn't, nor have thousands of other evangelical clergy who speak boldly, and often convincingly, about what the Bible says, and that is the point.

Declaring that "the Bible says" reveals a lack of understanding of the subjective nature of biblical study. James D. Smart, a biblical scholar of a past generation, called it our "interpretive context." Who we are is a composite of all the influences that have shaped our minds and hearts, all of which become constitutive of "hermeneutics," that is, biblical interpretation. Yet evangelicals refuse to acknowledge this unavoidable subjectivity, dismissing the fact that what a text means to them may not be at all what it actually means. It is similar to an eyewitness to a crime insisting that what she saw happen is what happened even though someone else witnessing the same crime says something entirely different happened.

Perceptions are always subjective. The search for truth begins when that subjectivity is acknowledged. Religion turns bad when the search for truth is usurped by the need for certainty, a point Peter Enns makes forcefully in his book, *The Sin of Certainty*. It is a memoir of sorts as he describes his personal journey to freedom of thought that cost him his teaching position at Westminster Seminary. He realized the folly of certainty when he was confronted by the truth that "life's challenges mock and then destroy a faith that rests on correct thinking and the preoccupation with defending it." Rather than losing his faith, though, he found it for the first time as he came to experience the truth that "life's challenges clear the clutter so we can see more clearly that faith calls for trust instead."[8] Certainty, he says, is not a sign that you have an unyielding faith in God. Rather, it means that

8 Enns, *The Sin of Certainty*, 116.

you have an unyielding faith in what you believe. In other words, he says, certainty is all about "trusting our beliefs rather than trusting God," something that is reflective of an Enlightenment perspective that evangelicals would be shocked to learn they hold. [9]

Certainty is not only the opposite of faith, it easily becomes a cradle for nurturing intolerance that births extremism. None of the ministers who said vile things after the Orlando shooting could have said what they did without having an overwhelming sense of certainty about what they believed. The possibility that they could be wrong never enters their minds. They don't know enough to know that they don't know, thus, they believe their own claims without realizing they are *nothing more than their own*. No amount of reason can take out of their minds what reason didn't put into it in the first place. That is what happens when knowledge doesn't matter, when ignorance (lack of knowledge) is not considered something to be overcome.

LOSING THEIR MIND

The primary reason education holds such little value among evangelicals, why fear lies behind inflexible beliefs that have little intellectual integrity, and why intolerance of diverse points of view is common, is because of a pervasive and insidious anti-intellectualism. Molly Worthen is convinced that evangelicalism is far more thoughtful and diverse than critics like me believe, even though she acknowledges that it has a "potent stream" of anti-intellectualism in it.[10]

In his 1964 Pulitzer Prize-winning book, *Anti-Intellectualism In American Life*, eminent historian Richard Hofstadter suggests anti-intellectualism is much more than a "stream" in evangelicalism. It was, he says, "the first arena for American intellectual life and thus the first arena for an anti-intellectual impulse,"[11] primarily because it promoted the view of religion as "largely an affair of the heart or of the intuitive qualities of the mind," thus "the rational mind is irrelevant or worse . . . barren or perhaps dangerous."[12]

9. Ibid., 21.

10. Worthen, *Apostles of Reason*, 2.

11. Hofstadter, *Anti-intellectualism in American Life*, 55.

12. Ibid., 47.

Evangelical scholar Mark Noll writes of evangelicalism's strong history of intellectual power that modern evangelicals have forsaken to the point of almost giving up any interest in thinking altogether. He describes evangelicals as having abandoned their commitment to critical thinking in the late nineteenth century because of the influence of fundamentalism.[13] He presents a comprehensive history, and I think an implicit defense, of the evangelical mind that once contributed to the rich tradition of Christian scholarship, but fell under the influence of the anti-intellectualism of a debilitating fundamentalism:

> ... I have argued that contemporary "evangelical thought" is best understood as a set of intellectual assumptions from the nineteenth-century synthesis of American and Protestant values and then filtered through the trauma of fundamentalist-modernist strife. Given that history, prospects for evangelical thought in the later twentieth century were no good . . . . The fundamentalist filter may have strained out enough atheism to preserve a kernel of supernatural Christianity, but for intellectual purposes, fundamentalism also strained out most of the ingredients required for the life of the mind.[14]

Two familiar expressions of fundamentalism's influence among evangelicals are biblical literalism and creation science. Literalism, Noll says, "reduced space for academic debate, intellectual experimentation, and nuanced discrimination between shades of opinion. The effect was to produce an anti-intellectualism by driving out intellectuals who "found modes of fundamentalism a disgrace."[15] The problem with fundamentalism, according to Noll, has been its "habits of the mind" that have undermined Scripture rather than unleashing the power of its message.[16] Creation science is an outgrowth of literalism that promotes a flawed method of reading the Bible that pits it against accepted historical and scientific knowledge. The creation stories in Genesis 1 and 2 that most scholars agree are different witnesses to God as Creator and author of life are, instead, used as a "scientific" counterpoint to evolutionary science.

Both literalism and creation science require evangelicals not only to believe a different story, but to reject established facts as if they are opinions

13. Ibid.

14. Noll, *The Scandal of the Evangelical Mind,* 211.

15. Ibid., 124.

16. Ibid., 177–208.

that some people believe and others don't. They reinforce the anti-intellec-tualism that has damaged evangelicalism's intellectual credibility, opening the door to extremists who exploit people's fears. That is what anti-intel-lectualism does. We encounter it every day, but don't necessarily see it for the danger it represents. Friends recently told me the story of attending the funeral of the father of one of their friends who belonged to an evangeli-cal church. At the end of the service the minister extended an altar call to anyone who was not a Christian. They would not, he assured them, ever see the man who had died in heaven unless they became a Christian because without that decision they would not be there.

I encountered it one morning when I answered the office telephone and a voice on the other end asked, "Are you the minister who wrote that letter to the newspaper supporting gay marriage?" I answered that I was. He immediately started quoting Leviticus 18:22, which says a man having sex with another man is an abomination to God, and then moved on to Romans 1:26–27, where Paul speaks of "unnatural" sexual relations, when I interrupted him to say that I was sure we were not going to agree on the is-sue so we may as well not have this conversation. That must have surprised him because he got very silent; then he finally said, "Well, then, I rebuke you in the name of Jesus."

No doubt the minister at the funeral and the layman who rebuked me were sincere, but that did not stop them from also being ignorant. To be "ignorant" literally means "lacking knowledge," as both of them did. Yet an-ti-intellectualists is a problem that actually goes much deeper than simply not knowing something. It is a disposition wherein a person consciously disdains the work of the mind. Hofstadter defined anti-intellectualism as "a resentment and suspicion of the life of the mind and those who are con-sidered to represent it," more of a common strain of attitudes and ideas bound together, he said, than a rigorous proposition.[17] His thesis was that most Americans were "non-intellectual" rather than anti-intellectual,[18] and that there was no truly "pure or unmixed" form of anti-intellectualism.[19] In fact, few intellectuals themselves, he said, "are without moments of anti-intellectualism," and "few anti-intellectuals without single minded intellectual passions."[20] Further, he said, in his experience he encountered

17. Hofstadter, *Anti-intellecutalism in American Life,* 7.

18. Ibid., 19.

19. Ibid., 21.

20. Ibid.

highly intellectual, learned people, who were at the same time anti-intellectual, including more than a few evangelical ministers, politicians, and
business people. But as common and unmixed as it may be, Hofstadter
believed that anti-intellectualism could give rise to "unqualified evil," like
the anti-Communist witch hunt of Wisconsin Senator Joseph McCarthy
in the 1950s, not least because it is often linked to good causes and could,
therefore, do great harm.[21]

Therein lies a cautionary word to us today. In the intervening fifty years
since Hofstadter's book was published, anti-intellectualism has reached the
point where ignorance itself has become a virtue in the minds of many
Americans, especially evangelicals. Even President Obama felt the need to
speak to this problem in his Rutgers University commencement address in
2016. "Let me be as clear as I can be: in politics and in life ignorance is not a
virtue. It's not cool to not know what you're talking about. That's not keeping it real or telling it like it is. That's not challenging political correctness.
That's just not knowing what you're talking about."[22]

That religion is promoting this kind of attitude is appalling on so many
levels, not least because there is growing evidence that anti-intellectualism
is fueling the culture of violence in the United States. Psychologists say
that anti-social behavior among young people like Dylan Roof, who shot
and killed the nine parishioners in a black South Carolina Church, has an
anti-intellectual element no one is paying attention to. Racism is an expression of anti-reason, a refusal to think through attitudes to recognize their
rational and irrational dimensions. In this kind of environment fear of the
other develops a life of its own that leads a person to act without thinking.
Anti-intellectualism is in fact the seedbed of irrational fear. In an article
posted on the *Psychology Today* website, attorney David Niose writes:

> What Americans rarely acknowledge is that many of their social
> problems are rooted in the rejection of critical thinking or, con-
> versely, the glorification of the emotional and irrational. What else
> could explain the hyper-patriotism that has many accepting an
> outlandish notion that America is far superior to the rest of the
> world? Love of one's country is fine, but many Americans seem to
> honestly believe that their country both invented and perfected
> the idea of freedom, that the quality of life here far surpasses ev-
> erywhere else in the world.

21. Ibid., 3.
22. Obama, "Remarks by the President."

But it doesn't. International quality of life rankings place America far from the top, at sixteenth. America's rates of murder and other violent crime dwarf most of the rest of the developed world, as does its incarceration rate, while its rates of education and scientific literacy are embarrassingly low. American schools, claiming to uphold "traditional values," avoid fact-based sex education, and thus we have the highest rates of teen pregnancy in the industrialized world. And those rates are notably highest where so-called "biblical values" are prominent. Go outside the Bible belt, and the rates generally trend downward. [23]

Niose thus concludes, "at the core of all of this dysfunction is an abandonment of reason."[24]

The scandal of evangelicalism is that it has perpetuated the belief that not thinking is good for faith while thinking is a threat. I would argue that this is one of the major reasons why evangelical partisanship has not been understood by evangelicals themselves as a threat to the very faith they hold dear. Supporting one political party because of oversimplified moral positions is appealing to people who don't like complexity or ambiguity. It takes work to think about applied morality in real life. It is almost as if the quest for certainty calms evangelical anxiety enough to make superficiality attractive. The goal is to be sure of what you know. Complexity, ambiguity, and diversity make that more difficult so they must be avoided. I once had a conversation with sisters who attended an evangelical church and who candidly admitted that they didn't care what scholars said about the Bible. They believed what they believed and that was enough for them. But it wasn't enough for all the gay couples in our state whose right to marriage the sisters opposed. It wasn't enough for the women in our state who wanted the right the sisters opposed to choose for themselves what to do about having an abortion. It wasn't enough for Muslims who the sisters believed were members of a religion that taught hate and condoned violence.

POLITICIZED RELIGION

The damage partisan evangelicalism has done to American politics is equaled by the impact it has had on Christianity itself. The American public has become skeptical of the integrity and intentions of all Christians

23. Niose, "Social dysfunction can be traced to the abandonment of reason."
24. Ibid.

because of evangelicalism's politicizing of the faith, especially in light of a history that includes Christian apathy towards and at times support of political oppression and atrocities. What happened in Germany during World War II is a sobering reminder of the dire consequences bad religion can cause.

As incredible as it seems, ordinary German Christians paid no attention to what was actually happening during Hitler's rise to power. The leaders in the "Faith Movement of German Christians" were nationalistic in their views and authored statements of faith that acknowledged Jesus Christ as Lord, but also pledged allegiance to the state. They made a "confessional commitment to the German people and its special history, to its authoritarian form of state, its Fuhrer, and its German race," is how scholar Eberhard Busch described their actions. Even "a centrist group" he described as less nationalistic made a public confession that "God has determined the fate of ethnicities and we recognize that God's leading in the ethnocentric renewal of our fatherland. We place ourselves in total love at the responsible service of the nation for which we are prepared to live or die." In short, as Busch noted, they confessed Jesus as Lord while also pledging loyalty to Hitler.[25]

The leaders of the Confessing Church of Germany called the German Christian confessions idolatrous. In 1934 they issued a Theological Declaration of Barmen, usually called the Barmen Declaration, authored primarily by Reformed theologian Karl Barth, declaring Jesus Christ only as the head of the church. It was intended to challenge the German Christians who were compromising their faith by putting service to Christ under the larger banner of service to the state. Barmen leaders believed this was nothing more than making the state at least equal to Christ, if not above him. Thus, they declared:

> We reject the false doctrine, as though the State, over and beyond its special commission [to provide justice and peace], should and could become the single and totalitarian order of human life, thus fulfilling the Church's vocation as well.
> We reject the false doctrine, as though the Church, over and beyond its special commission, should and could appropriate the characteristics, the tasks, and the dignity of the State, thus itself becoming an organ of the State.[26]

25. Busch, "The Barmen Thesis: Then and Now."
26. Barmen Declaration.

It was a turning point for both the leaders of the Confessing Church and the leaders of the German Christians, whose betrayal of their faith will live in infamy. The Holocaust was without question a singular event so horrific that it is unthinkable that such a thing could ever happen again. We can only hope and pray that is true, but I would argue that it is not overly dramatic to suggest that there is what evangelical scholar Charles Marsh calls a "theological comparison"[27] between what happened in Germany to what has happened to partisan evangelicals. The German people failed to understand the threat Hitler represented to everything German, including Christianity, a sobering reminder of how common it is for people of faith to miss moments when a historically tragic event is taking shape that will have lasting consequences. Jesus himself wept over Jerusalem's blindness to what was happening in his own day: "If you, even you, had only recognized on this day the things that make for peace! But now they are hidden from your eyes" (Luke 19:41).

For people of faith the danger is idolatry. Kings, rulers, and political parties want power and will do everything they can to hold on to it once they have it. The role of religion is to speak truth to that power, not to join hands with it. The prophets of ancient Israel like Amos, Hosea, Isaiah, Jeremiah, Ezekiel, and Micah emerged from nowhere to do precisely that. They dared to criticize Israel's kings for idolatry and social injustice (forgetting the poor and inhospitality to the stranger). They called on them to lead the nation back to faithfulness to Israel's only God, Yahweh, who demanded the practice of justice in caring for the poor and welcoming of the stranger. For their trouble they were thrown in jail and killed. Jesus knew the stories of what happened to them, prompting him to say, "Jerusalem, Jerusalem, the city that kills the prophets and stones those who are sent to it . . ." (Luke 13:34).

Ancient Israel was a theocracy, which means there is no exact parallel between it and our nation. But the need for people of faith to be willing to speak truth to power is never dependent upon historical circumstances. Truth and power always live in tension. This is why partisan evangelicalism is as dangerous for religion as it is for politics. Speaking truth to power requires a "prophetic distance" that minimizes the influence of power on the one who dares to speak. The moment evangelicals hitched their wagon to the Republican Party the need to speak truth to power became its first casualty.

27. Marsh, *Wayward Christian Soldiers,* 110.

Part of the seduction of power is that it convinces people of faith that they still have a voice on behalf of truth. It is common, therefore, for evangelicals to say that their position in the Republican Party is why they can speak prophetically. What they mean, of course, is that they can threaten to withdraw support from any Republican who refuses to hold the line against abortion and gay rights. That is why they support primary challenges to incumbents who make this mistake. They also believe that warning the nation against committing the sins of abortion, gay marriage, premarital sex, and accommodating the needs and wants of transgender persons is speaking prophetically. This only makes their claim of speaking truth to power all the more damning. "Prophetic" speech in the biblical tradition never justifies social injustice. Forgetting the poor is what produced Amos, Hosea, Isaiah, and Jeremiah. The prophet Micah summed up the entire prophetic tradition when he declared:

> He has told you, O mortal, what is good;
> and what does the LORD require of you
> but to do justice, and to love kindness,
> and to walk humbly with your God? (Mic 6:8)

This is the message evangelicals are reluctant to speak in Republican circles, choosing to pitch their tent in the camp of political operatives whose sole goal is to win elections, and thus, who are willing to say and do whatever serves that purpose. The review of the 2012 Republican Platform in the previous chapter clearly showed that when evangelicals chose to become Republicans they gave up the moral right to call the Party to attend to the demands of social justice. They were willing to limit their voice to personal morality. Injustice exists in America because it is the nature of our free society. People concerned about that injustice must serve as the voice of those who have no voice because they have no power. It is impossible to make the case that evangelicals are that voice except the few among them like Sojourners and Evangelicals for Social Action that have more influence among progressives than evangelicals.

Prophetic witness is not about changing the world. It is about speaking the best truth humans can know on behalf of the marginalized because of belief in God as the ultimate authority. Evangelicals have managed to convince themselves that standing for the unborn and fighting against "the gay agenda," they are being faithful to God. That might be believable if social justice issues captured their passion as well, rather than allowing their loyalty to Republicans to be their priority. What we see in partisan evangelicalism is an agenda that puts free market capitalism, gun rights, low taxes, small government, anti-immigration, and a strong military first. Everything else is second, strange as that might be for ostensible followers of the one who said to seek the kingdom of God first (Matt 6:33).

REQUIEM FOR BAD RELIGION

Bad religion hurts everybody, religious and non-religious alike. It ripples through every individual affected by it to others, many of whom become its unsuspecting victims. It is rooted in an unthinking radicalism that produces the vile words of partisan evangelicals we read and hear about in the news. It is a radicalism that is always a threat to faith and political civility. Name-calling matters; labeling people and political or religious views as "anti-God" has consequences; showing disrespect for people in public life, especially the President of the United States, should never be considered benign.

Couching such hate speech in the language of faith does not make it any less offensive or unacceptable. Evangelical sincerity does not transform it from bad religion to good. Nor does freedom of religion justify its existence. A tolerant society is not obligated to allow religious extremism to go unchallenged any more than it allows political extremism to go unchallenged. As a Christian I am dismayed by the image of Christians that partisan evangelicalism has created. It is common to hear people say that they don't want people they meet for the first time to know they are Christian because they don't want to be judged by the image evangelicals have created.

Despite the fact that it is more often true than not that what we learn from history is that we don't learn from it, we need a knowledge of history now more than ever. Documentary filmmaker Ken Burns made this point eloquently in his Stanford University Commencement address on June 12, 2016:

> I am in the business of memorializing—of history. It is not always a popular subject on college campuses today, particularly when, at times, it may seem to some an anachronistic and irrelevant pursuit, particularly with the ferocious urgency this moment seems to exert on us. It is my job, however, to remind people—with story, memory, anecdote and feeling—of the power our past also exerts,

to help us better understand what's going on now. It is my job to try to discern patterns and themes from history to enable us to interpret our dizzying, and sometimes dismaying, present.[28]

In that address he underscored the role history can and should play in our lives:

Each generation rediscovers and reexamines that part of its past that gives its present new meaning, new possibility and new power. The question becomes for us now—for you especially—what will we choose as our inspiration? Which distant events and long dead figures will provide us with the greatest help, the most coherent context, and the wisdom to go forward?[29]

It can do that, he says, "because the past often offers an illuminating and clear headed perspective from which to observe and reconcile the passions of the present moment, just when they threaten to overwhelm us."[30]

The illuminating power of the past is why critical thinking is essential to the quality of life we enjoy today and needs to be passed on to the next generation. Evangelicalism does not have to make for bad politics and bad religion. It once was a major voice in the human endeavor to be a good steward of the resources at our disposal to build a world that reflects the wisdom of choosing love over hate and oneness over division. Whether our country is or ever has been the last best hope on earth, as Lincoln said it was, is for history to decide. But Lincoln most assuredly knew of what he spoke when he said in his 1862 message to Congress: "The dogmas of the quiet past are inadequate to the stormy present . . . . [A]s our case is new, so we must think anew, and act anew. We must disenthrall ourselves, and then we shall save our country."[31]

We find ourselves less than a quarter of the way into the twenty-first century with the same threat of a divided house Lincoln faced, though for different reasons. So we must think anew, act anew, and disenthrall ourselves from the religious and political hubris in order to save our country in our own time in history. Bad religion needs to be buried by people who value the gift of the mind and believe in the capacity we possess as God's creation to make the world a good place. Partisan evangelicalism has done

28. Burns, "A House Divided Against Itself."

29. Ibid.

30. Ibid.

31. Lincoln, "Message to Congress."

enough damage to our politics and our religious heritage alike. It deserves to be rejected, for the sake of faith and American politics.

6

BORN AGAIN EVANGELICALISM

AMID THE VARIOUS DEFINITIONS and descriptions of evangelicalism we have cited, Angela Lahr suggests a very helpful one in her book, *Dreams and Apocalyptic Nightmares: The Cold War Origins of Political Evangelicalism*. Acknowledging the difficulty of the task for historians, especially since they cannot agree on what groups are and are not evangelical, she nonetheless offers as direct and clear a statement as any I have read. "Evangelicals generally define themselves as Christians who consider the scriptures as an essential guide for their personal and political lives."[1] While her book focuses on "millennial/apocalyptic-inspired evangelicalism and its involvement in politics,"[2] her simple statement points to a general characteristic that has certainly been true of partisan evangelicals since the founding of the Moral Majority. They do claim without equivocation that the Bible not only tells them how to live—it tells them how to vote.

Previously I noted that just before the 2004 presidential election Jerry Falwell Sr. told his congregation to "vote Christian," having made it clear that what he meant was "vote Republican" without coming right out and saying so. A story Angela Lahr recounts in her book confirms that he was not always subtle about convoluting faith and Republican politics. In 2004 Tavis Smiley did an interview with Jerry Falwell Sr. and Jim Wallis on National Public Radio. They were discussing the issue of evangelical "values" with Falwell focused on personal morality and Wallis on social morality. Falwell suggested that Wallis may not be the evangelical he thought he was. They exchanged passionate responses when a seemingly exasperated

1. Quoted in Marsh, *Wayward Christian Soldiers*, 5.
2. Ibid.

Falwell finally asked Wallis: "Did you vote for Al Gore last time? . . . Did you vote for Ronald Reagan? . . . Did you vote for George Bush Sr.?" Wallis admitted that he had not voted for any of them, to which Falwell responded that he thought Wallis was "about as evangelical as an oak tree."[3]

Falwell's comment reflected a mind-set prevalent in evangelicalism that may have be a key factor in Charles Marsh attaching the phrase, "Freeing the Gospel from Political Captivity," as the subtitle to his provocative book, *Wayward Christian Soldiers*. Speaking as an evangelical and a scholar, Marsh criticized attempts to align the Christian faith with any political party or person, something he saw to his dismay in evangelical statements that characterized George Bush's 2004 victory over John Kerry as "a gift of Providence" and a "miraculous deliverance."[4] An evangelicalism that gave de facto support to Bush's preemptive Iraq War that killed thousands of innocent men, women, and children was sufficient reason in his mind to suggest that "it would be better for Christians to stand in solidarity with compassionate atheists and agnostics, firmly resolved against injustice and cruelty, than to sing 'Amazing Grace' with the heroic masses who cannot tell the difference between the cross and the flag."[5]

Marsh's book is a compelling exposition of basic evangelical faith that is focused on teaching the nations about the gospel of Christ by living it instead of politicizing it, an evangelicalism that learns how to stop being so noisy and begins to listen.[6] His is an evangelicalism that arises from Scripture instead of using it to support Republican policy positions. For evangelicals like Marsh, the notion that to "vote Christian" would mean voting Republican or Democratic borders on blasphemy.

Undeterred as they are, partisan evangelicals have persisted in playing politics with their faith. Much to their dismay and disgust, the Supreme Court of the United States has been forced to remind them that government is not in the business of endorsing religious beliefs. Most of the "morals regulation" victories evangelicals have enjoyed have been short lived for not meeting constitutional muster. That in turn has made partisan evangelicals more committed to electing a Republican president who would make Supreme Court and federal bench appointments more to their liking. From an evangelical perspective, "activist judges" are standing in the way of their

3. Ibid.
4. Ibid., 3.
5. Ibid., 14.
6. Ibid., 151.

moving the country as close as it can be to a Christian theocracy without disregarding the Constitution entirely. Partisan politics is for them a means to an end, not the end itself, and, therefore, is not a vice or a threat to religion or politics. Just the opposite. They believe it is the salvation of both.

Despite what evangelicals believe, since the ratification of the Constitution in 1787, our nation has sought to balance the tension between religion and democracy, including freedom of thought/choice and community moral standards. At times we have lived in peace and harmony and at times we have experienced civil war, civil unrest, and civil disobedience. In certain moments we have been unified and at others we have appeared ready to dissolve the union that makes us the United States. In all these moments evangelicals have done little to contribute to reconciling efforts; instead they have tried to blur the line between church and state.

Surveys show that most Americans have a sort of collective bipolar attitude toward evangelicals. To a large extent, without being as dogmatic as evangelicals are, a large portion of them consider themselves to be quite religious. Nearly three-quarters say they pray regularly, say their faith is very important to them, and believe many of the same things evangelicals believe.[7] That is not surprising since basic evangelical beliefs reflect the major tenets of what Protestant and Catholic churches have taught people to believe for centuries, especially the centrality of believing in the death and resurrection of Jesus as the only means of salvation. What separates evangelicals from the rest of the Christian population, however, is their *rigidity of beliefs*. Most evangelicals, for example, believe in clear and absolute standards of moral conduct, whereas 64 percent of the general population believes right and wrong depends on the circumstances or situation.[8]

As you would expect, most Americans do not agree with the inflexible political attitudes of evangelicals on moral issues either, not least because they believe in the right of every American to think for himself or herself. In addition, they are suspicious of civil or religious authority that wants to impose limits on that freedom. This accounts for the fact that a majority not only support *Roe v. Wade*, they identify themselves as "pro-choice."[9] The death of Justice Antonin Scalia in 2016 dealt a blow to the hopes of evangelicals who had come to believe that they had finally gotten a Supreme Court friendlier to its moral agenda with the last two George W. Bush

7. Pew Research, "U.S. Public Becoming Less Religious."
8. Pew Research, "Belief in absolute standards for right and wrong.."
9. Gallup Poll, "Americans Choose 'Pro-Choice' for First Time in Seven Years."

appointments of Justices Roberts and Alito. With one more appointment they would have the solid conservative majority needed to have state moral legislation upheld. Uneasy with the way Justice Kennedy voted on issues such as the Defense of Marriage Act, gays in the military, and same-sex marriage, they were wanting another true conservative to be the next appointment. Then Scalia died of a heart attack under a liberal Democratic president and their hopes seemed doomed.

Nothing on the political landscape shows hope that Republicans in Congress are ready to move beyond gridlock to actually doing the nation's business, especially since evangelicals have doubled down on their intention to use their political power in the way they believe is to their advantage. They played a pivotal role in Donald Trump gaining the 2016 Republican presidential nomination, not without paying a price, though. As noted in Chapter 1, it caused considerable controversy among evangelicals who, because of who Trump was, saw support for him as an example of politics prevailing over religious principles.

In all the ways partisan evangelicals have been a problem for politics and religion, the one persistent issue continues to be their attitude of non-compromise. They appear as if they would rather go down in defeat or grind the legislative process to a halt before reaching an agreement with the opposition. Given the peculiar form of democracy that is America, this simply does not work. In a parliamentary system the majority party rules until the electorate chooses to switch sides. It sometimes forces a winning party to forge an alliance with one or more smaller parties in order to form a ruling majority in parliament. Once that is done, the Prime Minister, who is the leader of the winning majority party, leads the government. Legislation is decided by a simple majority vote. But in the Republican form of democracy, we have a president who may not be a member of the party with a Congressional majority. Moreover, in the Senate the minority party holds considerable power with the filibuster that has in recent years created the need of a sixty-vote supermajority to break it. Therein lies the procedural reason for our present dysfunctional government. Without genuine concern by all for the well-being of the nation, legislation cannot be passed. Moreover, the president's veto power requires a two-thirds majority vote in both the Senate and the House to be overridden. Not surprisingly, it seldom happens.

The *bad politics* evangelicals have helped to create in our country is what most Americans see, but behind it is the *bad religion* partisan evangelicalism represents. Doing something about that has to be the first step toward a change for the better. What that will entail is what I mean by the title of this chapter, "born again evangelicalism." The term "born again" describes the decisive change evangelicals believe anyone can (and must) experience through conversion. Believing in the atoning death of Jesus on the cross for your sins and accepting him as your Lord and Savior is, they say, like experiencing a new birth. Baptism by immersion that symbolizes dying to the old life and rising to the new one seals this "born again" experience.

This is what partisan evangelicalism urgently needs—being "born again," perhaps again and again. Since the 1970s evangelicals have not improved the political or the religious environment of the nation. Just the opposite. We have become less religious rather than more and less civil in our discourse on public policies, to the point where we are a house divided against itself. Although evangelicals are not solely responsible for these problems, they have played a major role in creating them. The fact that they are Christian places an extra burden on them to engage in a serious moral inventory of themselves. If evangelical leaders were willing to call their people to this kind of introspection, being "born again" might become more than just a catch phrase.

To enhance the chance of serious introspection, I suspect that part of what stands in the way of evangelicals being "born again" is that most of their leaders do not understand or, if they understand, do not appreciate the distinction Hofstadter made between intelligence and intellectualism. He described *intellect* as "the critical, creative, and contemplative side of the mind," whereas *intelligence* "seeks to grasp, manipulate, re-order, adjusts." The *intellect* "examines, ponders, wonders, theorizes, criticizes, and imagines," while *intelligence* "will seize the immediate meaning in a situation and evaluate it."[1] An intellectual is not someone who lives in an "ivory tower" away from the real world. He or she is simply someone, Hofstadter said, who has a dedication to the life of mind similar to a religious commitment, not least because, as he reminds us, clerics were the first to comprehend "the ultimate value in existence."[2]

Many evangelicals are intelligent, but they have also abandoned the life of the mind and in the process lost their appreciation for the place of the intellect in spiritual growth and development. The joy of learning, of

1. Hofstadter, *Anti-intellectualism in American Life,* 25.
2. Ibid., 27.

studying, of experiencing the power of great ideas has been replaced by doctrine, dogma, and success. One way for the future to be different is for evangelical leaders to discover afresh that knowledge has intrinsic value because it is the key to deeper insights into and reverence for the meaning of existence. Practically this will help them teach and preach in ways that will lead their congregations to grow beyond being a community of believers to being a community of thinkers whose members have eyes that truly see and ears that truly hear.

LEARNING FROM HISTORY

Nothing is more helpful to change than learning from the past. For evangelicals such learning can begin with understanding how they got involved in "morals regulation" in the first place, as documented by John Compton's book, *The Evangelical Origins of The Living Constitution*. At least they might realize that legislating morality has never been an effective method for raising the moral standards of a community, and certainly not a nation. This insight could encourage evangelical leaders to refocus their energies on how to influence their own people to live the kind of life they want the whole nation to live. We have cited surveys that show unambiguously that evangelicals talk better than they live, something not at all unusual for religious people. Moral standards begin with families, the very institution evangelicals say they want to protect, except they focus on other people's families instead of their own.

Next to their families their churches are the obvious place to spend their energies on being a moral community. Pastors could teach and preach about the biblical imperative of social justice as a way to show devotion to God. They could encourage church members to think for themselves as they weigh what political candidate should get their vote by examining everything he or she stands for rather than a single issue. In addition, congregations are where pastors could teach about the dangers of evangelicals making political alliances with Republicans (or Democrats), or what Charles Marsh calls "freeing the gospel from political captivity."[3] Family and churches are the places to teach morality instead of looking to schools, court houses, or government to do it. In short, families and congregations are where evangelicals could teach themselves and their children how to

3. Marsh, *Wayward Christian Soldiers*.

be Christian in modern America without trying to force their beliefs on everyone else.

The second history lesson that could help them in this process of change is to accept, however begrudgingly, the facts about the nation's founding. The number of times evangelicals say America was founded as a Christian nation will never make it true. History is what it is, as Princeton historian Kevin Kruse documents in his book, *One Nation Under God: How Corporate America Invented Christian America*. That history is that the idea of America as a Christian nation is a myth born of a mid-twentieth-century marketing scheme created by corporate interests in order to promote American capitalism.[4] It is not that our founders did not believe in God, or that many of them were not Christians. It is the fact that they consciously *chose* to maintain a separation between church and state that protected both.

American belief in this separation is why most Americans do not support the morality laws evangelicals persuade Republican state legislators to pass. They may agree with the intention, but also possess enough common sense to know that people embrace moral standards only as they make sense to them, and no amount of external authority will ever change that fact. For morality to be real, it must first be embraced willingly. That should be instructive to evangelicals about the most effective way they might go about changing the world for the better.

One of the first signs that evangelicals were learning from history would be a more thoughtful response to Supreme Court decisions. While they might still disagree with them, they could at least acknowledge the Court's effort to render fair and balanced decisions consistent with its reading of the Constitution. At the very least they might not persist in making claims demonstrably false. The June, 2016 Supreme Court decision in *Whole Woman's Health et al. v. Hellerstedt* presented an opportunity for them to do that. The issue was a sweeping law restricting abortions passed by the Texas Legislature in 2013 that required doctors who perform abortions to have admitting privileges at a hospital no more than thirty miles from the abortion clinic and required abortion clinics to meet the same health and safety standards as ambulatory surgical centers that perform much more complicated procedures. The justification of the law was that it was necessary to protect women's health.

4. Kruse, *One Nation Under God*, 11.

Opponents argued that women's health was not at risk and that these restrictions were unnecessary. They were intended, instead, as a back door way to shut down most abortion clinics in Texas that could not possibly meet these requirements. The Court agreed. Writing for the majority Justice Stephen Breyer said: "At the same time, the record evidence indicates that the requirement places a 'substantial obstacle' in a woman's path to abortion. The dramatic drop in the number of clinics means fewer doctors, longer waiting, and increased crowding." The ruling went on to say: "The record contains adequate legal and factual support for the District Court's conclusion that the admitting-privileges requirement imposes an 'undue burden' on a woman's right to choose."[5] The ruling acknowledged once again what the court had said in the past, that states can regulate abortion, but only if laws do not place an undue burden on women seeking access. It also noted that the state of Texas has not presented any evidence supporting the claim that the new law would provide essential healthcare protection for women having an abortion. In her supporting opinion, Justice Ruth Bader Ginsburg stated that the new law could have the opposite effect, that in light of the previous circumstances that existed before the new law was passed, "it is beyond rational belief that [it] could genuinely protect the health of women." Further, she wrote: "When a State severely limits access to safe and legal procedures, women in desperate circumstances may resort to unlicensed rogue practitioners."[6]

This is the same approach the Supreme Court has used since the early 1900s. Under the Constitution states can engage in "morals regulation" as long as the laws they pass do not violate individual constitutional rights. History shows clearly that the American judiciary has consistently refused to do precisely what evangelicals accuse judges of doing—legislate from the bench. It might change evangelicals and the nation if they were willing to accept the necessity of the balanced tension the courts have tried to maintain. It would help if they realized that people who don't agree with them on moral issues are just as moral as they are. It might help them see that not achieving everything they want does not prevent them from attaining some of it, that some is better than none at all. It seems at least plausible that a more informed grasp of American history could result in evangelicals undergoing a significant change in attitude.

5. *Whole Woman's Health et al. v. Hellerstedt.*
6. Ibid.

Evangelicals have enjoyed some "morals regulation" victories through TRAP laws, and have elected Senators and Representatives who do their bidding in Congress, indicative that they still have sufficient influence among Republicans to continue promoting a no compromise attitude that reaches beyond moral issues to anything they oppose. At the end of the day, though, when they look at the big picture of what they have achieved, they will see that abortion remains a legal right, gay marriage is now the law of the land, the courts have declared creation science a religious teaching rather than legitimate science, and religious freedom laws have produced a backlash from many quarters, including the business community. Any way that they look at the impact they have had, it should be unmistakably clear that at best their successes have been short lived, that in reality they have little to show for their political involvement except to make it difficult for government to work.

IS CHANGE REALISTIC?

Any hope or optimism about the changes I am suggesting depends, of course, on evangelicals reclaiming the tradition of critical thinking. Thinking is not everything, but nothing of much lasting value happens without it. But is it realistic to think the evangelical community can take the gift of the mind seriously again? Evangelical scholar Mark Noll says probably not. "Can a Christian mind develop out of American evangelicalism?" he asks. "Based solely on twentieth century historical precedent, it does not seem likely."[7] Yet he holds out a glimmer of hope that evangelicalism might rediscover that it is called to engage the world with "the mind of Christ" and that Christian scholarship holds the key to equipping themselves for that purpose.[8]

One of the steps he suggests to this end would be for evangelicals to begin distinguishing between what is "distinctive" to American evangelicalism and what is "essential" to Christianity, subordinating the former to the latter. Evangelical distinctiveness has to do with beliefs about the Bible, for example, while essentials have to do with the message of the Bible. Distinctiveness has to do with activism while essentials have to do with gratitude to God that may give rise to contemplation and study as well as activism.

7. Noll, *The Scandal of the Evangelical Mind*, 241.

8. Ibid., 243.

Distinctiveness has to do with crisis conversion, while essentials have to do with living a whole life committed to God.[9]

That is a demanding challenge for a community of Christians who have no recent history of valuing the mind even as they have devoted time and resources in the service of partisan politics. It has been twenty-three years since Noll's book was published with little evidence thus far that it has had any tangible influence on evangelical pastors and church members. If his cogent message has reached anyone it has been the best of the gifted evangelical scholars whose own reach has been limited. The fact is partisan evangelicalism has gotten worse rather than better in the intervening years. The hope for "born again" evangelicalism depends on evangelicals maturing in their faith. Knowing history will have a primary impact on that possibility.

Finally, there is at least one other thing that could help in this process—a measure of spiritual humility. "Blessed are the meek," Jesus said. The "meek" are those who manifest *praus*, humbleness, a gentle spirit. They inherit or take possession of the earth, the land, the space they occupy (Matt 5:5). Evangelicals are like the rest of us in needing humility, gentleness of spirit. Underneath an uncompromising attitude is an unconscious arrogance that gets in the way of relationships. It is easy to spot. The presumption that they can speak for God is a dead giveaway.

Humility would help them see that speaking about God as if they are God is a form of idolatry. Practically it separates evangelicals from others in an "us vs. them" tension. Humility, on the other hand, creates a less combative worldview. It would be an acknowledgement that they accept their limitations as fallible human beings, including the comprehension of truth, making what they believe less dependent on being right. Hubris imposes a terrible burden where the weight of the world and the future of humankind rests on their shoulders. Humility is the doorway to gratitude for life, to living well without the need to live perfectly. And it makes genuine trust in the goodness of God more possible.

Should evangelicals undergo the changes I am suggesting, they might well come to understand that embracing neighborliness is the goal of Christianity to which nothing else compares or stands as equal. Not that it is an easy goal to reach. Neighborliness takes all the energy anyone can muster because loving others is the most difficult thing anyone can do. We humans talk about love as if it is easy to do when we know that it isn't. All

9. Ibid., 243–44.

of us struggle to love others, even those closest to us, and certainly those who live near us who we wish would move away. On top of that Jesus cuts us no slack. He not only told us to love our neighbor, he added "enemies" to the list. "You have heard that it was said, 'You shall love your neighbor and hate your enemy.' But I say to you, love your enemies and pray for those who persecute you" (Matt 5:43-44).

Damn! The words of Jesus always have the power to bring us up short. I have enough trouble loving my neighbor whose yard looks like an episode of *Sanford and Son*. Expecting me to love terrorists who want to kill me, my family, my friends, seems like a bridge too far. Yet his words are there and every interpretation I have given to them brings me back to square one. *I am to love my enemies and my neighbors*. Perhaps the path to that level of spiritual maturity is the final challenge to evangelicals, a call to trust in God's love more than their own ability to save the world.

BIBLIOGRAPHY

Adams, Brooks. "New Utah AG: Cost to defend same-sex marriage ban worthwhile." *The Salt Lake Tribune*, December 31, 2013. http://archive.sltrib.com/story.php?ref=/sltrib/news/57332678-78/state-court-utah-attorney.html.csp.

Agiesta, Jennifer. "Support for SCOTUS hearings remains strong, CNN/ORC poll finds." CNN, March 25, 2016. http://www.cnn.com/2016/03/25/politics/merrick-garland-supreme-court-nominee/.

American Civil Liberties Union. "Reconciling Faith and Evolution in the Classroom: A Conversation with Susan Epperson, 42 Years Later." 2010. https://www.aclu.org/reconciling-faith-and-evolution-classroom-conversation-susan-epperson-42-years-later.

Anderson, Dan. "'Enough is Enough' declares Elon Commencement speaker David Gergen." E-Net News, May 21, 2016. http://www.elon.edu/E-Net/Article/132946.

Associated Press. "Parents, schools divided as sex ed controversy erupts." CBS News, January 19, 2016. http://www.cbsnews.com/news/sex-education-controversy-erupts-in-omaha/.

Bailey, Sarah Pulliam. "From Franklin Graham to Tony Campolo, some evangelical leaders are splitting over gay marriage." *The Washington Post*, June 9, 2015. https://www.washingtonpost.com/.

Barmen Declaration. http://www.sacred-texts.com/chr/barmen.htm.

"Barna Group survey exposes Evangelical Christians strongly oppose marriage equality." Episcopal Café, September 5, 2015. http://www.episcopalcafe.com/barna-group-survey-exposes-evangelical-christians-strongly-oppose-marriage-equality/.

Barnes, Robert. "Case weighing religious freedom against rights of others is headed to Supreme Court." *The Washington Post*, March 2, 2014. https://www.washingtonpost.com/politics/case-weighing-religious-freedom-against-rights-of-others-is-headed-to-supreme-court/2014/03/02/88de86d4-a198-11e3-b8d8-94577ff66b28_story.html.

———. "Stevens says Supreme Court decision on voter ID was correct, but maybe not right." *The Washington Post*, May 15, 2016. https://www.washingtonpost.com/politics/courts_law/stevens-says-supreme-court-decision-on-voter-id-was-correct-but-maybe-not-right/2016/05/15/9683c51c-193f-11e6-9e16-2e5a123aac62_story.html?hpid=hp_hp-more-top-stories_highcourt-433pm%3Ahomepage%2Fstory.

Bauman, Michael. "Law and Morality." The Christian Research Institute. http://www.equip.org/article/law-and-morality/.

Bean, Lydia. *The Politics of Evangelical Identity*. Kindle edition. Princeton, NJ: Princeton University Press, 2016.

Berman, Mark. "Oklahoma legislature passes bill making it a felony to perform abortions." *The Washington Post*, May 20, 2016. https://www.washingtonpost.com/news/post-nation/wp/2016/05/19/oklahoma-legislature-passes-bill-making-it-a-felony-to-perform-abortions/.

Bernstein, Jonathan. "All Filibusters, All the Time." *BloombergView*, May 9, 2014. https://www.bloomberg.com/view/articles/2014-05-09/all-filibusters-all-the-time.

Bever, Lindsey. "Pastor refuses to mourn Orlando victims: 'The tragedy is that more of them didn't die.'" *The Washington Post*, June 15, 2016. https://www.washingtonpost.com/news/acts-of-faith/wp/2016/06/14/pastor-refuses-to-mourn-orlando-victims-the-tragedy-is-that-more-of-them-didnt-die/.

Bivins, Jason. *The Religion of Fear*. Kindle edition. New York: Oxford University Press, 2008.

Bolling, Bill. "What to call a do-something conservative?" *Richmond Times Dispatch* online, Saturday, March 26. http://www.richmond.com/zzstyling/view-oped-nosig/article_fb387809-fbad-571f-9279-171dc48c0fd0.html.

Boyd, Greg. *The Myth of a Christian Nation: How the Quest for Political Power Is Destroying the Church*. Grand Rapids, MI: Zondervan, 2007.

Brooks, David. "The Governing Cancer of Our Time." *New York Times*, February 26, 2016. http://www.nytimes.com/2016/02/26/opinion/the-governing-cancer-of-our-time.html?mwrsm=Facebook&_r=0.

Bumpas, Bill. "What are evangelicals' thoughts on election issues?" OneNewsNow, August 7, 2015. http://www.onenewsnow.com/church/2015/08/17/what-are-evangelicals-thoughts-on-election-issues.

Burk, Denny. "Three Observations about Tony Campolo's acceptance of committed gay relationships." A commentary on theology, politics, and culture, June 8, 2015. http://www.dennyburk.com/three-observations-about-tony-campolos-acceptance-of-committed-gay-relationships/.

Burns, Ken. "A House Divided Against Itself." *HuffPost*, June 12, 2016. http://www.huffingtonpost.com/ken-burns/ken-burnss-commencement_b_10430204.html.

Busch, Eberhard. "The Barmen Thesis: Then and Now." 2004 Warfield Lecture, Princeton Theological Seminary, 2–3. www.worldcat.org/.../barmen-theses-then-and-now...2004-warfield-lectures.

Buttry, Stephen. "Candidates focus on Christian beliefs." *Des Moines Register*, December 15, 1999. http://www.cnn.com/1999/ALLPOLITICS/stories/12/15/religion.register/index.html?_s=PM:ALLPOLITICS.

Caldwell, Suzanna. "Cost to state of defending same-sex marriage lawsuit tops $100,000." *Alaska Dispatch News*, November 18, 2014. http://www.adn.com/article/20141118/cost-state-defending-same-sex-marriage-lawsuit-tops-100000.

Cason, Mike. "Roy Moore says probate judges have duty to enforce same-sex marriage ban." *The Huntsville Times*, January 6, 2016. http://www.al.com/news/index.ssf/2016/01/roy_moore_says_probate_judges.html.

Center for Science and Culture. "Intelligent Design." http://www.intelligentdesign.org/whatisid.php.

Chan, Melissa. "Tennessee hardware store owner posts 'No Gays Allowed' sign on front door: 'I'll never regret this.'" *New York Daily News*, July 1, 2015. http://www.nydailynews.com/news/national/tennessee-hardware-store-owner-posts-no-gays-allowed-sign-article-1.2277673.

Chappell, Bill. "House Approves Bill To Cease Funding Planned Parenthood." NPR, September 18, 2015. http://www.npr.org/people/14562108/bill-chappell.

Charles, Tyler. "The Secret Sexual Revolution: A recent study reveals most single Christians are having sex. We undress why." *Relevant*, February 20, 2012. http://www.relevantmagazine.com/life/relationship/features/28337-the-secret-sexual-revolution.

Clement, Scott. "Republicans embrace Trump's ban on Muslims while most others reject it." *The Washington Post*, December 14, 2015. https://www.washingtonpost.com/politics/americans-reject-trumps-muslim-ban-but-republicans-embrace-it/2015/12/14/24f1c1a0-a285-11e5-9c4e-be37f66848bb_story.html.

Coffin, William Sloane. Lecture delivered at Lexington Theological Seminary, Kentucky.

Colb, Sherry F. "The New Mexico Supreme Court Applies Anti-Discrimination Law to Wedding Photographer Refusing to Photograph Same-Sex Commitment Ceremonies." Verdict, September 4, 2013. https://verdict.justia.com/2013/09/04/new-mexico-supreme-court-anti-discrimination-law-to-wedding-photographer.

Collins, Francis. *The Language of God: A Scientist Presents Evidence for Belief.* New York: Free Press, 2006.

Compton, John. *The Evangelical Origins of the Living Constitution.* Kindle edition. Cambridge, MA: Harvard University Press, 2014.

Conan, Neal. "In Politics, Sometimes The Facts Don't Matter." *Talk of the Nation*, NPR, July 13, 2010. http://www.npr.org/templates/story/story.php?storyId=128490874.

Coontz, Stephanie. *Marriage, a History: How Love Conquered Marriage.* New York: Penguin, 2006. Quoted in "History of Marriage: 13 Surprising Facts," by Tia Ghose, Live Science, June 26, 2013, www.livescience.com/37777-history-of-marriage.html.

Cotterell, Bill. "Rick Scott Signs Abortion Restrictions Law." *Huffington Post*, March 28, 2016. http://www.huffingtonpost.com/entry/rick-scott-florida-abortion_us_56f6e6d5e4b0143a9b4869dc.

Council on American-Islamic Relations (CAIR). *A Brief Overview of the Pervasiveness of Anti-Islam Legislation.* January, 2013. https://www.cair.com/images/pdf/Pervasiveness-of-anti-Islam-legislation.pdf.

Coutts, Sharona. "Texas Spends Nearly $650,000 Defending Anti-Choice Laws." Rewire, January 21, 2014. https://rewire.news/article/2014/01/21/texas-spends-nearly-650000-defending-anti-choice-la.

Danforth, John C. Religion & Politics. A project of the John C. Danforth Center, Washington University in St. Louis. http://religionandpolitics.org/about-us/.

Dean, John. *Conservatives Without Conscience.* New York: Penguin, 2007.

"Democrats at the Sojourners Forum." *New York Times*, June 4, 2007. http://www.nytimes.com/2007/06/04/us/politics/04text-dems.html.

Diamond, Jeremy. "Ted Cruz: Police need to 'patrol and secure' Muslim neighborhoods." CNN, March 22, 2016. http://www.cnn.com/2016/03/22/politics/ted-cruz-muslim-neighborhoods/.

Dias, Elizabeth. "Donald Trump's Prosperity Preachers: Meet the evangelical outsiders who are flocking to the Republican's campaign." *Time*, April 15, 2016. http://time.com/donald-trump-prosperity-preachers/?xid=emailshare.

Dionne, E. J. *Why the Right Went Wrong: Conservatism—From Goldwater to the Tea Party and Beyond.* New York: Simon & Schuster, 2016.

Domonoske, Camila. "Alabama Chief Justice Orders Judges To Enforce Ban On Same-Sex Marriage." NPR, January 6, 2016. http://www.npr.org/sections/thetwo-way/2016/01/06/462161670/alabama-chief-justice-orders-state-to-enforce-ban-on-same-sex-marriage.

Dreher, Rod. "Democrats as the Anti-Christian Party." *The American Conservative,* February 12, 2015. http://www.theamericanconservative.com/dreher/democrats-as-the-anti-christian-party/.

———. "How Bobby Jindal Wrecked Louisiana." *The American Conservative,* February 6, 2015. http://www.theamericanconservative.com/dreher/how-bobby-jindal-wrecked-louisiana/.

Ehrenreich, Barbara. "Disease of Our Making: Wars produce warlike societies, which in turn make the world more dangerous." *Los Angeles Times,* March 23, 2003. http://articles.latimes.com/2003/mar/23/news/war-opehrenreich16.

Einenkel, Walter. "Survey Finds That Christians Have the Most Abortions in U.S." Alternet, December 2, 2015. http://www.alternet.org/belief/christian-groups-survey-finds-christians-have-most-abortions-us.

Elliott, Emory. Foreword to *The Puritan Origins of American Sex.* Edited by Tracy Fessenden, Nicholas F. Radel, and Magdalena J. Zaborowska. New York: Routledge, 2001.

Enns, Peter. *The Sin of Certainty: Why God Desires Our Trust More than Our Correct Beliefs.* New York: HarperOne, 2016.

Epperson v. Arkansas. The U.S. Supreme Court Case 393 U.S. 97, (no. 7). Argued: October 16, 1968, Decided: November 12, 1968, Legal Information Institute of the Cornell University Law School. https://www.law.cornell.edu/supremecourt/text/393/97.

Esposito, John. "It's The Policy Stupid: Political Islam and US Foreign Policy." Georgetown School of Foreign Service. https://acmcu.georgetown.edu/the-policy-stupid.

Evangelicalbeliefs.com. http://www.evangelicalbeliefs.com/.

Falsani, Cathleen. "Why Tony Campolo's LGBTQ Reversal is Evangelicalism's Tipping Point." *Religious Dispatches,* June 10, 2015. http://religiondispatches.org/why-tony-campolos-lgbtq-reversal-is-evangelicalisms-tipping-point/.

Ford, Zack. "How A New Book About Gay Christians Is Reviving Evangelical Homophobia." ThinkProgress, April 23, 2014. (http://thinkprogress.org/lgbt/2014/04/23/3429818/matthew-vines-southern-baptist/.

———. "North Carolina Just Lost 400 Jobs Because Of Its Anti-LGBT Law." ThinkProgress, April 5, 2016. http://thinkprogress.org/lgbt/2016/04/05/3766501/paypal-north-carolina/.

Frum, David. "Don't Knock the Reform Conservatives." *The Atlantic,* July 10, 2014. https://www.theatlantic.com/politics/archive/2014/07/dont-knock-the-reform-conservatives/374247.

Funk, Cary, and Becka A. Alper. "Religion and Views on Climate and Energy Issues." Pew Research Center, October 22, 2015. http://www.pewinternet.org/2015/10/22/religion-and-views-on-climate-and-energy-issues/.

Gallup Poll. "Americans Choose 'Pro-Choice' for First Time in Seven Years." Gallup, May 29, 2015. http://www.gallup.com/poll/183434/americans-choose-pro-choice-first-time-seven-years.aspx.

Gates, Jimmie E. "Miss. law allows churches to train members to pack heat." *USA Today,* April 15, 2016. https://www.usatoday.com/story/news/politics/2016/04/15/mississippi-guns-churches-law/83096512/.

Geewax, Marilyn. "Atlanta Businesses Again Lead Push Against Social Conservatives." NPR, March 29, 2016. http://www.npr.org/sections/thetwo-way/2016/03/29/472198269/atlanta-businesses-again-lead-push-against-social-conservatives.

Gibson, John. *The War On Christmas: How The Liberal Plot to Ban The Sacred Christian Holiday Is Worse Than You Think*. New York: Penguin, 2005.

Gill, Sam. Statements Bill O'Reilly made in a discussion with Neal Cavuto November 30, 2005. Fox News, *Media Matters*, December 1, 2005. http://mediamatters.org/video/2005/12/01/oreilly-brought-christmas-war-to-cavuto/134335.

Gillman, Howard, Mark A. Graber, and Keith E. Whittington. "American Constitutionalism, Supplementary Material, The Contemporary Era—Democratic Rights/Equality/Equality Under the Law." *Elaine Photography, LLC v. Willock*, 309 P.3d 53–NM 2013.

Goodnough, Abby, and William Yardleymarch. "Federal Judge Condemns Intervention in Schiavo Case." *The New York Times*, March 31, 2005. http://www.nytimes.com/2005/03/31/us/federal-judge-condemns-intervention-in-schiavo-case.html?_r=0.

"GOP's Favorability Rating Edges Lower." Pew Research Center: US Policy and Politics, April 28, 2016, http://www.people-press.org/2016/04/28/gops-favorability-rating-edges-lower/.

Greeley, Andrew. "Senator Bradley's Religion: The American presidency desperately needs a return to privacy, even including religious beliefs." Beliefnet, February 23, 2000. http://www.beliefnet.com/news/2000/03/senator-bradleys-religion.aspx.

Grunwald, Michael. "The Party of No: New Details on the GOP Plot to Obstruct Obama." *Time*, August 23, 2012. http://swampland.time.com/2012/08/23/the-party-of-no-new-details-on-the-gop-plot-to-obstruct-obama/.

Hannity, Sean. *The Sean Hannity Show*, April 2, 2015. http:forums.hannity.com/showthread.php?2456083-The-Democratic-Party-Has-Officially-Become-The-Anti-Christian-Party.

Hauerwas, Stanley. "Abortion, Theologically Understood." Posted on LifeWatch, 1991. http://lifewatch.org/abortion.html.

Hauserdec, Christine. "Wheaton College Professor Is Put on Leave After Remarks Supporting Muslims." *The New York Times*, December 16, 2015. http://www.nytimes.com/2015/12/17/us/wheaton-college-professor-larycia-hawkins-muslim-scarf.html?.

Healym, Melissa. "Scientists find DNA differences between gay men and their straight twin brothers." *Los Angeles Times* online, October 8, 2015. http://www.twinsfoundation.com/twinsblog/2015/10/scientists-find-dna-differences-between-gay-men-and-their-straight-twin-brothers-los-angeles-times-63/.

Hiestand, Gerald. "Evangelicals, Premarital Sexual Ethics, and My Grocery List." *First Things*, August, 14, 2012. http://www.firstthings.com/web-exclusives/2012/08/evangelicals-premarital-sexual-ethics-and-my-grocery-list.

Hofstadter, Richard. *Anti-intellectualism in American Life*. Kindle edition. New York: Vintage, 1966.

Horgan, John. "Climate Change: Facts Versus Opinions: When it comes to climate change, can 'facts' be distinguished from 'opinions'?" *Scientific American*, October 1, 2015. http://blogs.scientificamerican.com/cross-check/climate-change-facts-versus-opinions/.

Hunter, James Davison. *Cultural Wars: The Struggle To Define America*. Kindle edition. New York: Basic, 1992.

Idelman, Shane. "5 Ways Tony Campolo and Others Miss the Bible Mark With New Views on Gay Christians." Charismatic News, June 11, 2015. http://www.charismanews.

com/opinion/50057-5-ways-tony-campolo-and-others-miss-the-bible-mark-with-new-views-on-gay-christians.

Indiana Religious Freedom Law. *IndyStar*, April 2, 2015. http://www.indystar.com/story/news/politics/2015/03/27/text-indianas-religious-freedom-law/70539772/.

Jones, Jeffrey M. "Atheists, Muslims See Most Bias as Presidential Candidates." Gallup Poll, June 21, 2012. http://www.gallup.com/poll/155285/atheists-muslims-bias-presidential-candidates.aspx.

Jones, Judge John E., III, the United States District Court For The Middle District of Pennsylvania, Tammy Kitzmiller, et al.: Case No. 04cv2688, plaintiffs. (Dover Area School District, et al., Defendants: Memorandum Opunion, December 20, 2005).

Kaplan, Esther. *With God On Their Side: George W. Bush and the Christian Right*. New York: The New Press, 2005.

Kennedy, Anthony. *Obergefell et al.* Supreme Court of the United States. Argued April 28, 2015—Decided June 26, 2015. https//www.supremecourt.gov/opinions/14pdf/14-556_3204.pdf.

King, Martin Luther, Jr. *Where Do We Go From Here: Chaos or Community*. New York: Harper & Row, 1967.

Kinnaman, David. "How Americans View 'Evangelical Voters.'" Research Releases in Culture & Media, The Barna Group, September 9, 2008. https://www.barna.org/barna-update/media-watch/24-how-americans-view-evangelical-voters#.V44llbFTFjo.

Klatch, Rebecca. *Women of the New Right: Women in the Political Economy*. Philadelphia: Temple University Press, 1987.

Kruse. Kevin, *One Nation Under God: How Corporate America Invented Christian America* Kindle edition. New York: Basic, 2016.

Kurtzeleben, Danielle. "Planned Parenthood Investigations Find No Fetal Tissue Sales." NPR News, January 28, 2016. http://www.npr.org/2016/01/28/464594826/in-wake-of-videos-planned-parenthood-investigations-find-no-fetal-tissue-sales).

Langer, Gary. "Poll: No Role for Government in Schiavo Case." ABC News, March 21, 2005. http://abcnews.go.com/Politics/PollVault/story?id=599622&page=1.

Liasson, Mara. "Conservative Advocate." NPR Morning Edition, May 25, 2001. http://www.npr.org/templates/story/story.php?storyId=1123439.

Langer, Gary. "Poll: No Role for Government in Schiavo Case." ABC News, March 21, 2005. http://abcnews.go.com/Politics/PollVault/story?id=599622&page=1.

Lincoln, Abraham. Second Annual Message to Congress, December 1, 1862. http://www.presidency.ucsb/edu/ws/?pid=29503.

Linn, Jan G. "Faith-based politics: An exchange: On not mimicking the religious right." *The Christian Century*, July 24, 2007. https://www.christiancentury.org/article/2007-07/faith-based-politics-exchange-1.

Lipka, Michael. "U.S. religious groups and their political leanings." Pew Research Center, February 2, 2016. http://www.pewresearch.org/fact-tank/2016/02/23/u-s-religious-groups-and-their-political-leanings/.

Lipka, Michael, and John Gramlich. "5 facts about abortion." FactTank: News in the Numbers, Pew Research Center, March 1, 2016. http://www.pewresearch.org/fact-tank/2017/01/26/5-facts-about-abortion/.

Loving v. Virginia. Legal Information Institute, Cornell University Law School. https://www.law.cornell.edu/supremecourt/text/388/1.

Machiavelli, Niccolò. *The Prince*. New York: Dutton, 1968.

————.*The Discourses on the First Decade of Titus Livius.* NP: CreateSpace, 2012.

Mann, Thomas, and Norman Ornstein. *The Broken Branch: How Congress Is Failing America and How to Get It Back on Track.* New York: Oxford University Press, 2008.

————.*It's Even Worse Than It Looks: How the American Constitutional System Collided With the New Politics of Extremism.* New York: Basic, 2012.

Marsh, Charles. *Wayward Christian Soldiers: Freeing the Gospel from Political Captivity.* New York: Oxford University Press, 2007.

Masci, David. "5 key findings about faith and politics in the 2016 presidential race." Pew Research Center, January 27, 2016. http://www.pewresearch.org/fact-tank/2016/01/27/key-findings-faith-and-politics-in-2016-presidential-race/.

Mathias, Christopher. "An American Muslim Kid's Message To Her Country." *The Huffington Post,* June 3, 2016. http://www.huffingtonpost.com/entry/muslim-kid-message-to-america-japanese-incarceration_us_57503378e4b0eb20fa0cd743.

McCain, John. "Floor Statement by Senator John McCain on Senate Intelligence Committee Report on CIA Interrogation Methods." Posted on the Senator's official website. https://www.mccain.senate.gov/public/index.cfm/2014/12/floor-statement-by-sen-mccain-on-senate-intelligence-committee-report-on-cia-interrogation-methods.

McLanahan, Sara, and Gary Sandefur. *Growing Up with a Single Parent: What Hurts, What Helps.* Boston: Harvard University Press, 1994.

Merritt, Jonathan. "Defining 'Evangelical': Its meaning has shifted throughout Christianity's long history and changes depending on who you ask, Why?" *The Atlantic,* December 7, 2015. http://www.theatlantic.com/politics/archive/2015/12/evangelical-christian/418236/.

Milbank, Dana. "Ted Cruz's phony Obamacare filibuster was really about … Ted Cruz." *The Washington Post* online, September 25, 2013. https://www.washingtonpost.com/opinions/ted-cruzs-phony-obamacare-filibuster-was-really-about-ted-cruz/2013/09/25/b8f273a8-2632-11e3-b3e9-d97fb087acd6_story.html.

Minnite, Lorraine C. "The Misleading Myth of Voter Fraus in American Elections." Scholar Strategy Network, January, 2014. http://www.scholarstrategynetwork.org/brief/misleading-myth-voter-fraud-american-elections.

Monk, John. "Barbecue eatery owner, segregationist Maurice Bessinger dies at 83." *The State* online, February 24, 2014. http://www.thestate.com/news/business/article13839323.html.

Mooney, Chris. "'And then we wept': Scientists say 93 percent of the Great Barrier Reef now bleached." *Washington Post,* April 20, 2016. https://www.washingtonpost.com/news/energy-environment/wp/2016/04/20/and-then-we-wept-scientists-say-93-percent-of-the-great-barrier-reef-now-bleached/.

Mouw, Richard. *Political Evangelism.* Grand Rapids, MI: Eerdmans, 1973.

Murphey, Cayle. "Most U.S. Christian groups grow more accepting of homosexuality." FactTank, December 16, 2015. http://www.pewresearch.org/fact-tank/2015/12/18/most-u-s-christian-groups-grow-more-accepting-of-homosexuality/.

Nasaw, Daniel. "Obama overturns Bush policy on stem cell research." *The Guardian,* March 9, 2009. https://www.theguardian.com/world/2009/mar/09/obma-administration-stem-cell-funding.

National Association of Evangelicals. "Resolution: Bioethics and Stem Cell Research." http://nae.net/bioethics-and-stem-cell-research/.

Newman v. Piggie Park Enterprises, Inc., 390 U.S. 400 (1968), Justia, U.S. Supreme Court. https://supreme.justia.com/cases/federal/us/390/400/case.html.

Niose, David. "Social dysfunction can be traced to the abandonment of reason." *Psychology Today,* June 23, 2015. https://www.psychologytoday.com/blog/our-humanity-naturally/201506/anti-intellectualism-is-killing-america.

Noll, Mark. *The Scandal of the Evangelical Mind.* Grand Rapids, MI: Eerdmans, 1994.

Norto, Ron. "Unintended Consequences." The Concise Encyclopedia of Economics. http://www.econlib.org/library/Enc/UnintendedConsequences.html.

Nyhan, Brendan. "Voter Fraud Is Rare, but Myth Is Widespread." *The UpShot,* June 10, 2014. http://www.nytimes.com/2014/06/11/upshot/vote-fraud-is-rare-but-myth-is-widespread.html?.

Obama, Barack. "Remarks by the President at Commencement Address at Rutgers, the State University of New Jersey." The White House, Office of the Press Secretary, May 15, 2016. https://obamawhitehouse.archives.gov/the-press-office/2016/05/15/remarks-president-commencement-address-rutgers-state-university-new.

Parsons, Christi. "Obama says report shows CIA torture program at odds with U.S. values." *Los Angeles Times,* December 9, 2014. http://www.latimes.com/nation/la-na-torture-report-reaction-20141209-story.html.

Pew Research Center. "Belief in absolute standards for right and wrong." http://www.pewforum.org/religious-landscape-study/belief-in-absolute-standards-for-right-and-wrong/.

———. "GOP's Favorability Rating Edges Lower." April 28, 2016. http://www.people-press.org/2016/04/28/gops-favorability-rating-edges-lower/.

———. "How the Faithful Voted: 2014 Preliminary Analysis." November 5, 2014. http://www.pewforum.org/2014/11/05/how-the-faithful-voted-2014-preliminary-analysis/.

———. " The political preferences of U.S. religious groups." February 23, 2016. http://www.pewresearch.org/fact-tank/2016/02/23/u-s-religious-groups-and-their-political-leanings/ft_16-02-22_religionpoliticalaffiliation_640px-2/.

———. "The Religious Dimensions of the Torture Debate." Updated May 7, 2009. http://www.pewforum.org/2009/04/29/the-religious-dimensions-of-the-torture-debate/.

———. "Slim Majority of Americans Support Passing Stricter Gun Control Laws." Pew Religion Research Institute, August 15, 2012. http://publicreligion.org/research/2012/08/august-2012-prri-rns-survey/#.VxUsTJX2Zjp.

———. "Survey | Slim Majority of Americans Support Passing Stricter Gun Control Laws." August 15, 2012. http://publicreligion.org/research/2012/08/august-2012-prri-rns-survey/#.VxUsTJX2Zjp.

———. "U.S. Public Becoming Less Religious: Modest Drop in Overall Rates of Belief and Practice, but Religiously Affiliated Americans Are as Observant as Before." November 3, 2015. http://www.pewforum.org/2015/11/03/u-s-public-becoming-less-religious/.

Perlstein, Rick. "Why Conservatives Think the Ends Justify the Means: Who needs a majority—or democracy—when you just know that your cause is the most righteous?" *The Nation* online, April 8, 2013. https://www.thenation.com/article/why-conservatives-think-ends-justify-means/.

Pierce, Charles P. "Bobby Jindal Is Going Around Offering Advice While the State He Just Left Falls Apart." *Esquire,* March 4, 2016. http://www.esquire.com/news-politics/politics/news/a42714/bobby-jindal-louisiana/.

Posner, Sarah. "Christians More Supportive of Torture than Non-Religious Americans." *Religion Dispatches,* December 16, 2014. http://religiondispatches.org/christians-more-supportive-of-torture-than-non-religious-americans/..

———. *God's Profits: Faith, Fraud, and the Republican Crusade for Values Voters.* Sausilito, CA: PoliPointPress, 2008.

Poushter, Jacob. "In nations with significant Muslim populations, much disdain for ISIS." Pew Research Center, November 17, 2015. http://www.pewresearch.org/fact-tank/2015/11/17/in-nations-with-significant-muslim-populations-much-disdain-for-isis/.

Prager, John. "Christian Pastor Calls Orlando Massacre 'Good News' Because 50 'F*ggots' Died." Addicting Info, June 12, 2016. http://addictinginfo.org/2016/06/12/christian-pastor-calls-orlando-massacre-good-news-because-50-fggots-died-video/.

"Prohibition." History Online. http://www.history.com/topics/prohibition.

Quinlan, Casey. "Carly Fiorina Stubbornly Stands By Inaccurate Description Of Planned Parenthood Video." ThinkProgress, September 27, 2015. http://thinkprogress.org/politics/2015/09/27/3706123/carly-fiorina-defends-abortion-comments/.

"Quote for the Day." *The Atlantic,* November 24, 2006. http://www.theatlantic.com/daily-dish/archive/2006/11/quote-for-the-day/232168/.

Religious Freedom Restoration Act. http://prop1.org/legal/rfra.htm.

Rizzo, Tony. "Phil Kline is indefinitely suspended from practicing law." *The Kansas City Star,* October 18, 2013. http://www.kansascity.com/news/local/article329802/Phill-Kline-is-indefinitely-suspended-from-practicing-law.html.

———. "Phil Kline is indefinitely suspended from practicing law." *The Kansas City Star,* October 18, 2013. http://www.kansascity.com/news/local/article329802/Phill-Kline-is-indefinitely-suspended-from-practicing-law.html.

Rozsa, Matthew. "Inhofe says the Environmental Protection Agency is 'brainwashing our kids.'" *Salon,* March 16, 2017. http://www.salon.com/2017/03/16/global-warming-denier-james-inhofe-says-the-environmental-protection-agency-is-brainwashing-our-kids/.

Russell, Betsy. "Idaho to pay nearly $1M to plaintiffs for attorney fees in three cases." *The Spokesman-Review,* April 25, 2016. http://www.spokesman.com/blogs/boise/2015/aug/10/idaho-pay-nearly-1m-plaintiffs-attorney-fees-three-cases/.

Schmitt, Liz. "Talking to Evangelicals About Climate Change." *Soujouners,* March 2014. https://sojo.net/magazine/march-2014/talking-evangelicals-about-climate-change#sthash.4LNGdu7F.dpuf.

Scott, Dylan. "Boehner's Netanyahu Invite Is An 'Unprecedented' Diss Of Obama." *TPM,* January 21, 2015. http://talkingpointsmemo.com/dc/boehner-netanyahu-congress-invitation-obama.

Seitz-Wald, Alex. "The 'anti-God' party: You can't be a Christian and a Democrat at the same time, Virginia's GOP candidate for lieutenant governor says. *Salon,* Aug 1, 2013. http://www.salon.com/2013/08/01/virginia_lg_candidate_dems_are_anti_god/.

Sensenbrenner, Jim. "Suppress Votes? I'd Rather Lose My Job." *The New York Times,* Op-Ed, March 31, 2016. http://www.nytimes.com/2016/03/31/opinion/suppress-votes-id-rather-lose-my-job.html?_r=0.

Shelby County v. Holder, Attorney General, et al. Certiorari To The United States Court of Appeals For the District of Columbia Circuit, Section 4a–3, no. 12–96. Argued February 27, 2013—Decided June 25, 2013. http://www.supremecourt.gov/opinions/12pdf/12-96_6k47.pdf.

Smart, James D. *The Strange Silence of the Bible in The Church: A Study in Hermeneutics.* Louisville: Westminster John Knox, 1970.

Smidt, Corwin E. *American Evangelicals Today.* Lanham, MD: Rowman & Littlefield, 2013.

Stanley, Tiffany. "The Intellectual Civil War within Evangelicalism: An Interview with Molly Worthen." Religion and Politics, December 3, 2013. http://religionandpolitics. org/2013/12/03/the-intellectual-civil-war-within-evangelicalism.

Taylor, Jessica. "Citing 'Two Corinthians,' Trump Struggles To Make The Sale To Evangelicals." NPR, January 18, 2106. http://www.npr.org/2016/01/18/463528847/ citing-two-corinthians-trump-struggles-to-make-the-sale-to-evangelicals.

"'Tennessee hardware store puts up 'No Gays Allowed' sign." USA Today Network, WBIR-TV, Knoxville, TN, July 1, 2015. http://www.usatoday.com/story/news/nation-now/2015/07/01/tennessee-hardware-store-no-gays-allowed-sign/29552615/.

Tesfaye, Sophia. "Carly Fiorina and GOP frozen in denial over hoax video indictments." Salon.com, January 26, 2016. http://www.salon.com/2016/01/26/carly_fiorina_and_ gop_frozen_in_denial_over_hoax_video_indictments_planned_parenthood_has_ been_trafficking_in_body_parts/.

Tharoor, Ishaan Ishaan. "The case against Netanyahu's speech to Congress." *Washington Post,* March 2, 2015. https://www.washingtonpost.com/news/worldviews/ wp/2015/03/02/the-case-against-netanyahus-speech-to-congress/.

"The Governing Cancer of Our Time." *New York Times,* February 26, 2016. http:// www.nytimes.com/2016/02/26/opinion/the-governing-cancer-of-our-time. html?mwrsm=Facebook&_r=0.

Throckmorton, Warren. "Dr. Francis Collins comments on homosexuality and genetics." *Patheos,* September 21, 2008. http://www.patheos/com/blogs/ warrenthrockmorton/2008/09/21/dr-francis-collins-comments-on-homosexuality-and-genetics/.

Trinko, Katrina. "Will Mississippi's last abortion clinic close?" *National Review* online, December 18, 2012. http://www.nationalreview.com/article/335814/will-mississippis-last-abortion-clinic-close-katrina-trinko.

United States Supreme Court. *Roe v. Wade.* 1973, no. 70–18, Argued: December 13, 1971— Decided: January 22, 1973. http://caselaw.findlaw.com/us-supreme-court/410/113. html.

USA Today. "12 states still ban sodomy a decade after court ruling." *USA Today,* April 21, 2014. http://www.usatoday.com/story/news/nation/2014/04/21/12-states-ban-sodomy-a-decade-after-court-ruling/7981025/.

U.S. Supreme Court. *Epperson v. Arkansas.* (No. 7). Argued: October 16, 1968—Decided: November 12, 1968. https://www.law.cornell.edu/supremecourt/text/393/97.

Vines, Matthew. *God and the Gay Christian: The Biblical Case in Support of Same-Sex Relationships.* New York: Convergent, 2015.

Volsky, Igor. "17 Disgraceful Facts Buried In The Senate's 600 Page Torture Report." *ThinkProgress,* December 9, 2014. http://thinkprogress.org/ world/2014/12/09/3601312/17-disgraceful-facts-contained-in-the-torture-report/.

"Voter ID laws and the evidence: A report from the Government Accountability Office." Journalistic Resource, October 16, 2014. http://journalistsresource.org/studies/ politics/elections/voter-id-laws-empirical-evidence-government-accountability-office.

Wallis, Jim. "Faith-based politics: An exchange: Principled, not partisan, politics." *The Christian Century*, July 24, 2007. https://www.christiancentury.org/article/2007-07/faith-based-politics-exchange-2.

Warren, Elizabeth. "Going to Extremes: The Supreme Court and Senate Republicans' Unprecedented Record of Obstruction of President Obama's Nominees." http://big.assets.huffingtonpost.com/WarrenSCOTUSreport.pdf.

Wehner, Peter. "Why this elections makes me hate the word 'evangelical.'" *Washington Post*, February 29, 2016. https://www.washingtonpost.com/news/acts-of-faith/wp/2016/02/29/russell-moore-why-this-election-makes-me-hate-the-word-evangelical/.

———. "An Evangelical Christian Looks at Homosexuality." Patheos, June 11, 2013. http://www.patheos.com/blogs/philosophicalfragments/2013/06/11/evangelical-christian-looks-homosexuality-peter-wehner/.

Wellman, Jack. "Are Christians Republicans or Democrats? A Biblical Look at Politics." What Christians Want To Know. http://www.whatchristianswanttoknow.com/are-christians-republicans-or-democrats-a-biblical-look-at-politics/#ixzz4AHlZTeLf.

Whole Woman's Health, et al. v. Hellerstedt Commissioner, Texas Department of State Health Services, et al. Certiorari To The United States Court of Appelas for the Fifth Circuit. No. 15–274. Argued March 2, 2016—Decided June 27, 2016. http://www.supremecourt.gov/opinions/15pdf/15-274_p8ko.pdf.

Wihbey, John. "Voter ID laws and the evidence: A report from the Government Accountability Office." Journalist's Resource, Harvard Kennedy School Shorenstein Center on Media, Politics, and Policy, October 16, 2014. https://journalistsresource.org/studies/politics/elections/voter-id-laws-empirical-evidence-government-accountability-office.

Woods, Mark. "Evangelicalism is not about homophobia or hating women, says new Evangelical Alliance director." *Christianity Today*, December 16, 2014. http://www.christiantoday.com/article/evangelicalism.is.not.about.homophobia.or.hating.women.says.new.evangelical.alliance.director/44462.htm.

Worthen, Molly. *Apostles of Reason: The Crisis of Authority in American Evangelicalism.* Kindle edition. New York: Oxford University Press, 2013.

Wright, John. "'Death to Gays' Pastor Donnie Romero Threatens Violence Against LGBT Protesters." The New Civil Rights Movement, June 23, 2016. http://www.thenewcivilrightsmovement.com/johnwright/fort_worth_lgbt_group_responds_to_death_to_gays_pastor_with_fundraiser_for_homeless_youth.

Wuthnow, Robert. *Inventing American Religion: Polls, Surveys, And The Continuous Quest For Nation's Faith.* Kindle edition. New York: Oxford University Press, 2015.

Yardley, Jonathan. "Rule and Ruin" by Geoffrey Kabaservice, a book review. *Washington Post*, February 3, 2012. https://www.washingtonpost.com/entertainment/books/2012/01/18/gIQA9LtpnQ_story.html.

Young, Neil J. "Why evangelicals are attacking Pope Francis on Abortion." *The Huffington Post*, September 4, 2015. http://www.huffingtonpost.com/neil-j-young/evangelicals-attacking-pope-abortion_b_8082982.html.

YouTube. "Is This Young Boy the Future of Religion?" February 7, 2013. https://www.youtube.com/watch?v=1CjUHNYzW1E.

NAME INDEX

Hughes, Terry, 82
Huguenin, Elaine and Jonathan, 64,
	64–66
Hunter, James Davison, 24, 24n4
Hunter, Joel, 101
Hyde, Henry, 97

Idelman, Shane, 34n17
Inhofe, James (Jim), 7, 84
Isaiah, 129, 130

Jackson, E. W., 93
Jakes, T. D., 120
Jefferson, 21
Jeremiah, 129, 130
Jessen, Bruce, 73
Jesus, xiii, 16, 17, 21, 32–33, 68, 69,
	71, 101, 119, 120, 125, 128,
	129, 138, 143, 144
Jeter, Mildred, 29, 30
Jimenez, Roger, 118
Jindal, Bobby, 103–4
Johnson, Lyndon, 2
Jones, Jeffrey M., 59n22, 98n26
Jones, John E., 60–61

Kabaservice, Geoffrey, 9
Kaplan, Esther, 16–17, 17n40, 96
Kaplan, Rebecca, 97n24
Kennedy, Anthony, 27, 27n6, 137
Kerry, John, 96, 135
King, Martin Luther, Jr., 22, 87, 87n5
Kinnaman, David, 20n48
Klatch, Rebecca, 18, 18n42
Kline, Phil, 104–5
Kogut, Mary, 54
Kruse, Kevin, 140, 140n4
Kurtzeleben, Danielle, 52n4

Lahr, Angela, 134
Langer, Gary, 46n36
Laurie, Greg, 113
Liasson, Mara, 5n16
Lincoln, 101, 132, 132n31
Linn, Jan G., 100n31
Lipka, Michael, 41n26
Livingston, Robert, 97

Loving, Richard, 29, 30
Lynch, Loretta, 8

MacArthur, John, 113
Machiavelli, Niccolò di Bernardo dei,
	51, 51n1, 51n2
Mann, Thomas, 1n3, 3, 3n8, 4, 6n18,
	9, 9n25, 20n45, 23, 23n1
Marsh, Charles, 129n27, 134n1, 135,
	139, 139n3
Marshall, John, 90
Masci, David, 98n27
Mateen, Omar, 117
Mathias, Christopher, 110n52
Mbubaegbu, Chine, 12–13
McCain, John, 6, 74–75, 75n50, 87
McCarthy, Joseph, 109
McCarthy, Kevin, 3
McClellan, Mark, 97
McConnell, Mitch, 6, 8
McCorvey, Norma ("Jane Roe"),
	39–40
McLanahan, Sara, 36, 36n22
Mencken, H. L., 89
Merritt, Jonathan, 12n33
Merritt, Sandra, 52
Mica, John, 6
Micah, 129, 130
Milbank, Dana, 87n4
Mills, Gene, 103
Mims, Sam, 42
Minnite, Lorraine C., 78n55
Mitchell, James, 73
Mohler, Albert, 33–34
Monk, John, 62n27
Mooney, Chris, 82n61
Moore, Roy, 27–28
Moore, Russell, 13–14, 21, 21n50
Murphey, Cayle, 33n14

Nasaw, Daniel, 44n33
Netanyahu, Benjamin, 88
Newman, Anne, 61
Niose, David, 126–27, 127n23
Nishiura, Takako "Kit," 109–10
Noll, Mark, 15, 15n38, 61, 124,
	124n14, 142, 142n7

SUBJECT INDEX

abandonment of reason, 127
abortion
    doctor murdered for performing,
      104
    evangelicalism and, 37–42
    Jimmy Carter's view on, 19
    as legal, safe, and rare, 41
    as a moral decision, 92
    not just a church issue or a
      Christian issue, 39
    remaining a legal right, 142
    states having different laws on
      before 1973, 39–40
    as the top concern of evangelicals,
      20
abortion and emergency
      contraception, in tenth-grade
      lessons on birth control, 47
abortion clinics, 41–42, 140–41
absoluteness, 35
absolutes, 49
absolutist attitude, 11
abstinence, 48, 97
activism, of evangelicals, 12
"activist judges," 135–36
admitting-privileges requirement,
    141
AIDS, 97
Alabama, 27, 28, 78
Alaska, 105
America, as the home of the free, 110
American College of Obstetricians
    and Gynecologists, on TRAP
    laws, 42
American Evangelicalism Today
    (Smidt), 11
American Freedom Law Center, 108

American Laws for American Courts
    (ALAC) model, 108
American materialism, teachings of
    Jesus used to bless, 119
American Medical Association, on
    TRAP laws, 42
American Psychiatric Association,
    removed homosexuality as a
    mental disorder, 32
American Public Health Association,
    on TRAP laws, 42
American schools, avoiding fact-
    based sex education, 127
Americans
    "non-intellectual" rather than
      anti-intellectual, 125
    not agreeing with the inflexible
      attitudes of evangelicals on
      moral issues, 136
    not embracing any particular
      moral vision, 24
    not sharing the opinion that the
      Republican Party is God's
      choice, 97
    as pragmatic, 49
    skeptical of evangelical preachers,
      xiv
    supporting *Roe v. Wade*, 41
Amyx Hardware & Roofing Supplies,
    67
anti-Communist witch hunt, of
    Joseph McCarthy, 126
anti-gay marriage amendment, in
    Minnesota, 26, 27
anti-gay marriage initiative, 31
"anti-God," as a label, 131